American Mafia:
The Rise and Fall of Organized Crime
In LAS VEGAS

MARK W. CURRAN

Library House Books
Simi Valley, CA

Copyright 2021 – Mark W. Curran

All rights reserved. No part of this book may be reproduced in any format or by any means without written permission from the publisher. For Information, contact Library House Books, 2828 Cochran Street, Suite 285 Simi Valley, CA 93065.

Library of Congress Cataloging-in-Publication Data

American Mafia:
The Rise and Fall of Organized Crime In Las Vegas
Mark W. Curran

ISBN: 978-1-936828-68-5 (Softcover)

First Edition January 1, 2022

Photo Credits:
Las Vegas Visitors Bureau - Jim Rose
UNLV Archives and Special Collections
Getty Images
Corbis Images
Las Vegas Sun
Las Vegas Review Journal
Creative Commons
The National Archive
Las Vegas Historical Society

This book is dedicated to the members of law enforcement and the journalists who risked their safety to bring members of organized crime to justice.

TABLE OF CONTENTS
♠

FOREWORD	1
INTRODUCTION	6
THE EARLY YEARS OF LAS VEGAS	8
THE MAFIA COMES TO LAS VEGAS	18
THE MAFIA EXPANDS TO MORE CASINOS	35
LAS VEGAS BECOMES AN ENTERTAINMENT MECCA	50
TROUBLE IN PARADISE	70
THE FBI CLOSES IN: CONVICTIONS	84
THE MAFIA IN LAS VEGAS ENDS	106
CORPORATIONS TAKE OVER	123
LAS VEGAS BECOMES DISNEYLAND	143
THE LAST RESORT - THE FINAL CHAPTER?	157
APPENDIX I	167
APPENDIX II	176
RECOMMENDED READING	186
INDEX	188

FOREWORD
♠

When I first embarked on the journey of making a documentary film about the American Mafia, I knew very little about the subject. I've been a research journalist for a number of years and written books and made films on a variety of subjects. After completing my last book project, I was looking around for a topic that had historical significance yet one the modern public still had a keen interest in. As I looked at books and documentaries about the American experience, one topic kept coming up again and again.

That subject was organized crime.

Ever since gangsters took center stage back at the early part of the 21st century, people have been fascinated by the Mob; criminals and justice are still at the forefront of our national interest. It was a subject I too had always had an interest in, yet very little practical knowledge. One thing that did get my attention was that much of the subject matter that was available online and in print about organized crime had very high interest level from the public.

I decided to do some online research and see what I might find.

After spending some weeks getting a sense of how organized crime had gotten started in America, and, subsequently how it had grown over the years, I knew I had found a topic that was both fascinating as well as complex. It became apparent that if I were to make a documentary that were comprehensive in nature, it would end up a 16 hour mini-series! I needed to focus my efforts on one aspect of it.

The city of Las Vegas was the single focal point that drew me in the most.

The more I dug into the fascinating history of Las Vegas and the mafia's role in its growth, the more hooked I became. Thus, the subject for my first full-length documentary film had me in its grip and it turned out to be a wild ride.

The story of how organized crime built a city out of the dust of the desert and transformed it into a magnificent mecca of glitz, excess and decadence would be the one that would occupy me for nearly a year and a half of research and place me in touch with people on both sides of the law.

From a journalistic point of view, I came to the subject with fresh eyes and this I saw as an advantage to finding the story from a different perspective than from one who had spent nearly a lifetime involved in the subject matter, as many of my expert interviewees had.

As I gathered materials, read books and sought out experts in the field, I discovered a rich subculture of journalists, fans, reporters and scholars who had made the history of the mafia a lifelong passion. This surprised me, as did the high level of cooperation and help I received from many members of this community.

But even more surprising to me was learning that organized crime is still operating in all of our major cities, including Las Vegas in the form of foreign criminal networks originating in Russia, China and the Middle East. It was also surprising to learn that some of the crime families that made up the core of organized crime 'back in the day' are still, to some extent, active.

Another twist to me was learning that many members of the families of the organized crime figures who were major players in the rise and fall of the mob in Las Vegas were [and are still] waging war on one another from events that occurred many years ago and whose original players were long dead and gone.

As such, many of the surviving members of these families refused to go on the record for the documentary and the book. And while I believe the resulting film and book would have been much more comprehensive and potent with their participation, I respect their right to silence.

Omerta is still alive and well.

Another surprising twist in the Las Vegas Mafia story is that even now, all these years later, some of its history is being re-examined in new light and in some cases, re-written. As confidential documents have become public and once-silent witnesses have come forth with their own accounts (and in some cases, even written books) we are learning even more about the years when The Dons ruled glitter gulch.

As a case in point, I recommend anyone interested in this subject to read David Bowman's new book *Bringing Down Cullotta,* in which he challenges that Frank Cullotta turned informant for reasons which have not been disclosed until now.

I am ever grateful for the many people who helped in the making of this film.

The book is not meant to be comprehensive, rather it serves as an entry point and overview of the main tenets of how the mob started and grew Las Vegas and how they were either run out of town or were brought to justice. I will leave it to the authors of the many books written by those more knowledgeable than I to tell their stories in fuller detail.

The documentary, *American Mafia: The Rise and Fall of Organized Crime In Las Vegas,* is meant to entertain and to inform a lay audience and show the main signposts along the highway, while this book serves as an overview or companion guide to the film.

For a much deeper dive, I recommend the books by Selwynn Raab, and Dennis Griffin, as well as from our interviewees; Jeff Burbank and Michael Green. (Please refer to the Recommended Reading section of this book.)

I'd like to thank all of those who helped in the preparation of this book and the making of the documentary, with a special 'Thank You' to the Mob Museum in Las Vegas for help with and use of research materials which appear in this book as well as the film.

A special shout out to the special archive of the University of Las Vegas and the Las Vegas Visitors Bureau for their help in assisting with the finding of historic photos so vital to the telling of this story, and to Larry Henry and Gary Jenkins for not only appearing in the documentary and book, but for moderating their respective Facebook Pages and Groups for fact checking and insights.

The story of the mob is dynamic and ever-changing. Here's a look at how it all got started in a place they call Las Vegas.

Mark W. Curran
Los Angeles, CA.
11-1-21

INTRODUCTION
♠

Las Vegas Nevada. One of the most iconic cities in the world, Today it's the site of scores of glittering palace casinos that reach high into the night sky.

A place where fortunes are made and lost. Where the dreams of even the most downtrodden can come true in the turn of a card or a spin of the wheel. It's a place where any and all desires can be fulfilled. But behind Las Vegas's glittering facade hides a sinister and deadly history.

This book explores the rise and fall of organized crime in Las Vegas. I'll take you behind the scenes into the history of how the mafia infiltrated a small desert town and how it grew to become one of the most feared and powerful organizations in the West.

This book [and the documentary film on which this book is based] in no way glorifies organized crime. It simply attempts to tell the history of how it got started and how it flourished in Las Vegas – and how it ended.

I've interviewed many experts and authors in the field, as well as consulted with historians who were kind enough to share their extensive knowledge with me on a subject I knew little about before attempting this project.

To them I give my heartfelt appreciation, as well as to you, the reader, for your interest in wanting to learn a vital part of our great American history.

Chapter 1:

THE EARLY YEARS OF LAS VEGAS
♠

In its early years, Las Vegas was just a whistle stop on the way to someplace else. It was a cowboy town. Bolstered by abundant ground water, it was a popular oasis as travelers made their way across the hot and dusty desert. In 1919 Prohibition was ratified with all consumption, manufacturing and distribution of liquor banned.

But on Sept. 7, 1929 work began on the building of Boulder Dam, which brought hundreds of workers and their families to Las Vegas. In the following years, Las Vegas went from being a frontier boom town to a major western style gambling mecca.

As small gambling joints opened all along Highway 91, little did anyone know this was the humble beginning of what would later be known as the famous Las Vegas Strip.

In 1930 the Union Pacific Railroad connected Las Vegas to Boulder City and in 1931 The Nevada Legislature relaxed marriage and divorce laws and repealed its gambling ban.

This would open the door for legal gambling. Although prohibition was still in effect, many small enterprises served illegal liquor and speakeasy establishments sprung up all over the city.

MICHAEL GREEN:
Las Vegas Historian and Mob Expert

American Mafia: *Can you speak a bit about the early days of the Las Vegas Strip when it first all began as a boom town?*

Michael Green: *If the Strip has a birth date, it's April 3rd 1941. That's the day the El Rancho Vegas opened at the corner of what's now Sahara in the Strip. And it was a resort hotel because it had the rooms, the casinos and the amenities. It only had about sixty five rooms, which today isn't even the floor of one hotel casino in Las Vegas. But it was the beginning. And about a year and a half later comes the hotel named The Last Frontier. Now, if you think about it, you've got El Rancho Vegas Hotel, Last Frontier. The names tell you something their old west style. They have a* theme they're supposed to evoke the old West. Then along comes the Flamingo, which is supposed to be the luxury hotel. And that sets the strip on a different path thematically. And since the mob will end up running the Flamingo, it also is a different path in terms of ownership.

American Mafia: *How did organized crime begin in Las Vegas?*

Michael Green: *If you want to know how organized crime begins in Las Vegas, part of the question is what kind of organized crime are you thinking of? You can go back into the 20s, the prohibition era, when there is prostitution downtown in a red light district and there's bootlegging with prohibition. And there's a guy in Las Vegas, Jim Ferguson, who's sort of a low grade mobster. He's doing what you associate with the mob later in the thirties after gambling becomes legal and drinking is legal again. You do get some early types who might have some connections and a few who really did. But when you think about organized crime in Las Vegas, you really start thinking about it seriously in the 1940's. In the 40s, with the arrival of the syndicate connected to New York, called the 'old bug and Meyer mob' and the people who worked with them, whether they were in New York or elsewhere in the country. By the* late forties, you really have the mob getting entrenched in ownership of casinos in Las Vegas.

American Mafia: *Who was Guy McAfee and what role did he play in the early Las Vegas mob?*

Michael Green: *Guy McAfee is a fascinating character on a variety of levels. He was a vice cop in the L.A. Sheriff's Department. His wife supposedly was involved in running prostitution and he was involved in running illegal casinos. And in 1938, there are a couple of reform administrations in California. Earl Warren, later famous as the Chief Justice, becomes Attorney General and he starts running the gambling cruise ships out of the area. There's a new mayor in L.A., Fletcher Barron, who's shutting down casinos. McAfee and his allies start moving into Las Vegas. It's the closest spot for legal gambling. McAfee buys a little club on Highway Ninety One, and the club's called the Ninety One Club. He eventually sells it to build The Last Frontier, and he moves downtown. He opens the Golden Nugget, and he's associated with organized crime. There are people working on his story, and there is a lot more we're eventually going to know, but he's a bit opaque right now. But one of McAfee's contributions is bringing in the sort of L.A. crowd that was experienced and running gambling operations, and that's beneficial for running gambling in Las Vegas. The other story is that supposedly he was standing on Highway Ninety One and he noticed these cars coming in and out and the lights on the cars. And he said something like, allegedly, you know, this reminds me of a street I used to cruise in Southern California. The Sunset Strip. And supposedly that's the birth of the Las Vegas Strip as 'The Strip.'*

The following year the Pair-O-Dice Club opened on Highway 91, which later would be known as the famous Las Vegas Strip.

Frank Detra and Family

The man who owned the club was Frank Detra, who came to be known as Las Vegas's first mobster.

Another roadhouse, The Red Rooster opened a year after the Pair-O-Dice, a mile farther south on Highway 91, becoming the first club in the area seen by passing motorists.

Red Rooster on Hwy. 91

On May 5, 1931, the county issued the Pair-O-Dice's manager, Oscar E. Klawitter, a license to run a roulette table, a craps table, and a blackjack table. Weeks later, the club was opened to the public and would later be the target of raids by the Federal government.

Detra's club encountered problems with the U.S. government, which threatened to close it down because of their illegal alcohol sales. But unlike the Red Rooster, the Pair-O-Dice was not raided by Federal agents.

Throughout most of the 1930s, the Pair-O-Dice was the more successful of the two clubs. It featured gaming, live orchestras, singers, dancing, and Italian food.

Guy McAfee 1931

In the late 1930s Guy McAfee entered the picture. He was a former Los Angeles police captain who had amassed a small fortune soliciting payoffs from the bookmakers he was supposed to arrest.

> Guy McAfee, L. A. Gambling Czar, Seeks Las Vegas License; Transfer From Southland Rumored

He purchased Detra's roadhouse and renamed it the 91 Club. McAfee was considered one of LA's biggest underworld leaders, with reporters calling him The Al Capone of Los Angeles. His relocation to Las Vegas in 1939 was front-page news.

J. MICHAEL NIOTTA:
Mafia Expert and Author

If you look at the advertisements for the early casinos running up and down Fremont beginning in 1939, you had the Frontier El Rancho, The Pioneer and then later the Golden Nugget in 1946. All these places were associated with the mob and Guy McAfee's name came up a lot in those places.

Scherer Street is actually named for L.B. "Tutor" Scherer, a colorful character in Las Vegas' early history. Scherer was born in Kenosha, Wis., in 1879. It's unclear how he came to be known as Tutor, but it is known that he was part of the mob syndicate in Los Angeles before heading to Las Vegas. You'll also see names like Milton Farmer Page, Eddie Moelis, Chuck Addison. Well, this same group of gamblers and racketeers partnered in Los Angeles throughout the long stretch of prohibition, leading all the way into the close of the 1930s. They came to Las Vegas along with Guy McAfee and started operations and scams throughout the city in the early days. Scherer, along with Page, Addison and Bill Kurland, began operating the Pioneer Club in 1942. By then, Las Vegas' population had mushroomed from roughly 1,000 in 1910 to more than 8,400 in 1940. These days, the downtown establishment is best known as home to Vegas Vic, the hand-waving, "Howdy, podner" neon cowboy who had to lose about a foot in height to make way for the Fremont Street Experience canopy. Scherer later became president of the El Rancho Vegas, the ill-fated divorcee retreat at the southwest corner of Las Vegas Boulevard and Sahara Avenue. It burned to the ground in 1960. He had stakes in other casinos, including the Las Vegas Club, the Thunderbird and the Sahara.

It was during these early years the mob speculated that at the close of prohibition, Las Vegas would become a source of unlimited cash - and they were right. So began the gold rush that would bring organized crime to Las Vegas.

Chapter 2:

THE MAFIA COMES TO LAS VEGAS
♠

By the late 1940's the mob nationwide was looking for new opportunities for fast, easy, illegal money. They saw their opportunity in the boom town of Las Vegas.

It was a place that had grown from a dusty whistle stop to a thriving and promising new bonanza. By then the mob had taken control over illegal gambling, drugs and prostitution in major cities coast to coast.

It would not be long before the Mafia would turn their attention to glitter gulch.

In the early 1940s, Meyer Lansky and Benjamin "Bugsy" Siegel drove across the desert from Los Angeles to the dusty railroad stop called Las Vegas. With temperatures soaring near 115 degrees, the wires in their Cadillac melted.

"There were times when I thought I would die in that desert," Lansky is quoted as saying in "The Money and the Power." "Vegas was a horrible place."

Meyer Lanksy

Lansky initially had dispatched Siegel to Las Vegas to take control of racetrack bets humming over the wires. Contrary to legend, it was Lansky, not Siegel, who envisioned what Las Vegas would become.

MICHAEL GREEN

American Mafia: *When did Bugsy Siegel arrive in Las Vegas and what was his claim to fame in its early beginnings?*

Michael Green: *Bugsy Siegel apparently came to Las Vegas around nineteen forty one and how much of it was his idea? How much of it was his colleagues' idea? There's a lot we don't know. He didn't write an autobiography. He was not noted for doing an oral history or writing letters.*

Siegel arrives in Las Vegas, actually to be involved in the race wire business. The whole idea that you have all this betting on horse racing, a lot of it is tied to the mob. If you control the wire, you can control the bookies and you can control a lot of money. And he moves in and takes that over. He's also interested in casinos.

He allegedly tried to buy the El Rancho Vegas, and the owner said the people of Las Vegas have been too good to me to sell to the likes of Siegel, and he lived to tell about it, and then later sold it to a different mobster.

Siegel got in the business downtown, first with the El Cortez, and then The Flamingo. When you talk about the

Flamingo, there are different origin stories. There are those who say it was Siegel's idea. There are those who say he had nothing to do with its conception. There are people who come down in the middle.

Here's what we know. There was a Hollywood businessman, Billy Wilkerson. He owned The Hollywood Reporter. He owned some nightclubs like Ciro's and he wanted to build a hotel casino. Unfortunately, he also gambled and drank. And there's an old saying in the casino business, if you want to make money in a casino... Own it. Well, he lost a lot of money.

Now, Siegel invests... and other mobsters also invest. Eventually, Siegel takes it over. How much of it was him as a silent partner originally? How involved was he? Wilkerson's side would say not at all. Siegel's side would say, 'Oh, it was all him."

I think it was more Wilkerson than Siegel. But that said, Siegel gets involved in building The Flamingo and gets it built and gets it open.

American Mafia: *How and why was Bugsy Siegel murdered?*

Michael Green: *Bugsy Siegel's murder is technically still, according to the Beverly Hills Police Department, an unsolved case, and maybe the proof of that is that there are so many versions of how it must have happened.*
We know he gets shot while at the home of Virginia Hill.

We know there's a person with him who apparently just dives under the couch. Pretty much. But who did it and why? Everything from money being stolen from the Flamingo by Seigel and Hill allegedly to a rumor that it really had nothing to do with the Flamingo and that it was actually Virginia Hill's brother who resented his mistreatment of Virginia.

There are stories of people being hired to do it. We really don't know exactly who did it. And as I say, there are theories. And until it's solved, it looks increasingly to me like murder on the Orient Express, where everybody walked in the room and got one shot.

American Mafia: *Can you give some of your insights on how the mob took over the Flamingo after Bugsy Siegel's murder?*

Michael Green: *After Bugsy was killed? There was a line used by Robert Lacey, a biographer of Lansky, who said that the new owners walked in like generals mopping up after a coup and said, "Mr. Siegel's dead, we're in control."*

Now, of course, with Siegel there, the mob did have The Flamingo. But one of the problems you run into here is Siegel was not necessarily in the business side of the mob so much as the muscle side and might not always have listened to the business side.

The guys who come in, they've done their time with muscle, they've moved up that way. But they also are experienced in casinos, bookmaking, and various operations.

So they have a better business sense, I think, than Siegel did. And the Flamingo is an enormous success under their control. Siegel would have said "It was moving in the right direction under me. I had laid it out. Things are going to be fine."

Maybe they would have been. But you don't get the nickname Bugsy because you're considered even tempered. He hated the nickname. But it's pinned on him. And in business, you don't always want someone who gets a little, as they would say, 'bugs.'

Benjamin "Bugsy" Siegel was one of the most infamous and feared gangsters of his day. Born Benjamin Siegelbaum on February 28, 1906, to Russian Jewish immigrants in Brooklyn, New York, Ben resented and vowed to rise above the poverty surrounding him.

Bugsy Siegel, Gangster

He sought wealth, fame and power, and by the age of fourteen, Ben Siegel, as he had others call him, had already started his own gang.

Employing tactics that were a foreshadowing of what was to come, Siegel began his gang by offering, in return for regular payments for his services, to "protect" pushcart peddlers' carts and goods from the frequent burglaries and vandalism that plagued them. The unsuspecting and penniless cart owners would almost always initially turn down Siegel's offer.

Bugsy Siegel mug shot

Flying into a rage, Siegel would douse the carts in kerosene, light them on fire, and demand payment. The peddlers, having little choice, would pay Siegel, falling under his "protection."

Siegel was drawn to Las Vegas in 1945 by his interest in legalized gambling and off-track betting. In 1931 Gambling (including Race & Sports wagering) was legalized in Nevada. Bet slips were hand written, however, in the mid-1940s – Bugsy Siegel was technically the first race disseminator in the state. One of the features of this service was race information (entries, odds, results) – otherwise known as the 'Race Wire'.

The race wire played an important role in the evolution of horse racing and betting. Bookies could keep track of races and illegally place bets through the wire. The wire provided off track betters with horse racing results, and for a time, Bugsy Siegel controlled the wire business in Nevada and California.

El Cortez Hotel, 1941

Bugsy Siegel purchased The El Cortez hotel for $600,000, along with Meyer Lansky and Moe Sedway. They later sold it for a $166,000 profit. He supervised the opening of the Flamingo Hotel and spent lavish sums of money preparing it and a marketing campaign was launched to draw celebrities from Hollywood.

Flamingo Hotel, 1946

On December 26, 1946, Siegel opened the newly renovated Flamingo Hotel in Las Vegas. Comedian Jimmy Durante headlined the night's entertainment, with music by Cuban band leader Xavier Cugat. Some of "Bugsy" Siegel's Hollywood friends, including actors George Raft, George Sanders, Sonny Tufts and George Jessel were in attendance.

Newly-opened Flamingo Hotel

The grand opening of the Flamingo Hotel, however, was not a success. Bad weather kept many other Hollywood guests from arriving. And because gamblers had no rooms at the hotel, they took their winnings and gambled elsewhere.

The casino lost $300,000 in the first week of operation. Siegel and his New York partners had invested $1 million in a property already under construction by Billy Wilkerson.

Bugsy Siegel and Billy Wilkerson

Wilkerson was the owner of the Hollywood Reporter as well as some very popular nightclubs in the Sunset Strip. Wilkerson had wanted to recreate the Sunset Strip in Las Vegas, with a European style hotel with luxurious rooms, a spa, health club, showroom, golf course, nightclub and upscale restaurant. But he soon ran out of money due to the high cost of materials immediately after the war.

Billy Wilkerson

Two weeks after the grand opening, the Flamingo closed down. It re-opened March 1, 1947, as The Fabulous Flamingo. Siegel forced Wilkerson out in April, and by May, the resort reported a profit, but it wasn't enough to save Siegel.

Convinced that Siegel was on the take, it is widely believed that his partners in the mob had him killed while he was reading the paper June 20, 1947, at girlfriend Virginia Hill's Beverly Hills mansion.

Hill was in Paris, having flown the coop after a fight with Siegel 10 days prior, when a killer shot through the window with a .30 caliber military M1 carbine.

But who did it?

Bugsy Siegel murder headline

Jeff Burbank, an author and mafia historian, offered his own thoughts on it:

"Lots of people were angry with him, and so it's really difficult to know for sure. So many people had a motive to kill Bugsy Siegel. It's really difficult to decide on who actually did, but it probably had something to do with the East Coast mob, tired of his cost overruns and arrogance with their money invested in the Flamingo."

"Well," Burbank continues, "The story is that within minutes after him being killed, somebody must have called Las Vegas about it just minutes after the bullets hit him in the face and killed him. It was reported that Gus Greenbaum and Moe Sedway came into the casino and they said, 'we're taking over.'"

"The staff was shocked to hear about Siegel, but they wanted to make sure that everybody knew that regardless of Siegel's death, they were continuing on as a business."

ERIC DEZENHALL:
Book author and authority on Las Vegas crime

Why was Bugsy Siegel murdered? Bugsy Siegel's murder has never been solved, and there's lots of theories.

The most popular one is that he was killed by his partners, allegedly for stealing.

What's interesting is later in their lives, some people who would be in the know, namely Meyer Lansky, Jimmy Aiello and Sidney Korsak of Chicago, were absolutely adamant that he was not stealing from the Flamingo.

What he was doing was blowing budgets left and right and treating his investors horribly, even though the Flamingo ended up turning a profit before he was killed. What Meyer, Jimmy Aiello and Sidney Korsak told people privately is that what happened was one of Virginia Hill's girlfriend's brothers killed him because a few days before the murder, he had been beaten. Prior to this, Virginia Hill had been beaten within an inch of her life. She fled to Paris. Her brother was well aware that Siegel was in trouble with his friends and partners and decided to take it upon himself.

We'll never know, of course, but there were lots of things about the murder that didn't have the hallmarks of a traditional mob hit. And the thing is when you make lots and lots of enemies and lots of those enemies are aware that you have lots of other enemies, somebody may have taken it upon themselves just to do it themselves, and he wasn't missed afterward.

Gus Greenbaum, right, relaxes poolside in the late 1940s or early 1950s. Moe Sedway, center, was Greenbaum's fellow executive at the Flamingo Hotel. The man at left is Ben Goffstein.
COURTESY OF UNLV SPECIAL COLLECTIONS

After Siegel's murder, mob-connected managers Moe Sedway and Gus Greenbaum took over and made the Flamingo profitable. This group combined physical and business toughness.

It included longtime Phoenix bookmaker and veteran casino operator Gus Greenbaum, Moe Sedway, Minneapolis gambling veteran Davie Berman, and Ben Goffstein, who was involved in often violent newspaper circulation wars. Some had a history of violence, but all were experienced businessmen.

By the start of the 1950's, the stage was set for the American Mafia to make Las Vegas their own personal piggy bank. With increasing Federal pressure and changing laws limiting their reach and power, the mob needed a new playground. Sin City would not disappoint. It was the beginning of a new era in crime, one that would change the city of Las Vegas... forever.

Chapter 3:
THE MAFIA EXPANDS TO MORE CASINOS
♠

During the 1950s and 1960s, mobsters helped build the Sahara, the Sands, the New Frontier and the Riviera. Money from organized crime was combined with funds from more respectable investors.

Meyer Lanksy

Some of these included Wall Street banks, union pension funds, the Mormon Church and the Princeton University endowment. Tourists flocked to the resorts... eight million a year by 1954.

They were drawn by performers such as Frank Sinatra, Dean Martin and Elvis Presley, and by rows of slot machines and gaming tables.

Meyer Lansky known as the "Mob's Accountant", was a major American organized crime figure who, along with his associate Charles "Lucky" Luciano, was instrumental in the development of the National Crime Syndicate in the United States.

Lansky-Lineup

Associated with the Jewish mob, Lansky developed a gambling empire that stretched across the world. He was said to own points (percentages) in casinos in Las Vegas, Cuba, The Bahamas and London. Although a member of the Jewish mob, Lansky undoubtedly had strong influence with the Italian-American Mafia and played a large role in the consolidation of the criminal underworld.

Over the next two decades, almost every hotel-casino in Las Vegas had some connection to Lansky and his New York/Miami branch of organized crime.

Their builders often had run illegal casinos in various locations from Providence, Rhode Island, to Portland, Oregon; from Minneapolis, Minnesota, to Dallas, Texas.

They apparently under reported their earnings and sent money to Lansky and other eastern investors.

MICHAEL GREEN

American Mafia: *Who was Meyer Lansky? And what was his role in organized crime in Las Vegas?*

Michael Green: *Meyer Lansky was kind of the secretary of the Treasury of Organized Crime. I like to say I've often thought if Lansky came along today, I'd put him in charge of the Federal Reserve or something, and all of our economic problems would be solved.*

He had a head for figures. He was a good diplomat. He grew up on the streets of New York, met Siegel when they were kids, and Lansky would get beaten up, would talk people out of beating above, got into gangs, got involved in various forms of thuggery. But he was the money man, and he was, in a sense, Siegel's diplomatic representative. If you've ever seen the movie Bugsy, there's a scene where Lansky is saying to Siegel something like 'Ben, you're becoming famous. Famous is good for Joe DiMaggio. It's not good for you.'

Well, it's kind of how Lansky approached things. We're here to make money. We're going to make money. Everybody needs to behave. And he'd broker the differences. So you had people like Frank Costello, Lucky Luciano, who might technically be considered the boss or Uber boss. But to me, Lansky is really the guy who makes it go.

Eric Dezenhall weighs in on Lansky: "Meyer Lansky has the reputation as the mob's accountant, which is kind of silly because there were lots of mobs and they didn't really need an accountant. He was also called the chairman of the board of the National

Crime Syndicate, which is kind of cute because there really wasn't such a thing as a crime syndicate."

"But," Dezenhall says, "There were a series of syndicates that came together when they had to. The best description of Meyer was that he was like a CEO of a large portfolio company. If you accept that the mob was a large private equity fund and that one of their biggest, their largest legitimate investments were in casino gambling."

"Meyer Lansky ran that it was his job to raise the money, to manage the money and to make certain that people who were competent were not only running the hotels and casinos, but were responsible for distributing what was known as 'The Skim' which were the unreported, non-taxed profits from the casinos that went out to mob bosses across the country, as well as to banks around the world for money laundering purposes."

GUS GREENBAUM RISE AND FALL

Gus Greenbaum, 1952

As a syndicate leader in Las Vegas, Gus Greenbaum was placed in charge of running the Flamingo. Greenbaum would order the deaths of Anthony Brancato and Anthony Trombino for robbing a syndicate hotel, the murder was carried out by Los Angeles crime family soldier Jimmy "the weasel" Fratianno.

Deaths of Anthony Brancato and Anthony Trombino

But Greenbaum was a man who had developed a few problems that had placed him at odds with his mob brothers.

Greenbaum's worsening gambling, womanizing, and drug habits eventually caused him to begin skimming from casino operations. His embezzlement was discovered by the Chicago Outfit.

On December 3, 1958, Greenbaum and his wife Bess were found dead in their Phoenix home. Their throats had been cut with a butcher knife.

MICHAEL GREEN

American Mafia: *Can you tell us any stories about Gus Greenbaum and Moe Sedway?*

Michael Green: *Gus Greenbaum and Moe Sedway end up owning the El Cortez downtown together. And the guy originally built, the El Cortez, also built the Thunderbird, and for some reason, allies of Meyer Lansky ended up with both of them. And that's the thing. Greenbaum comes out of Phoenix, where he's been involved in bookmaking. Sedway comes out of New York. He drove the prohibition era trucks for Siegel and Lansky. But they're together running this because this is a sort of national or even international conglomerate. It's organized crime. They're pretty organized. Now, Greenbaum goes on to be the head man really at the Flamingo. He wants to retire, and they use their powers of persuasion, apparently killing a family member to get him to come out of retirement and run the Riviera after it's built. Eventually, he's murdered. And to this day, there's a debate because it was a messy murder and his wife was killed and usually a professional hitman isn't messy and doesn't have to kill other family members. So there is a theory that it was just totally unrelated* because Greenbaum was also a drug addict, and that was a problem for the mob. Because if you're involved in drug addiction, is there a chance that you're going to give away the goods? Is there a chance you're going to talk there? You're going to mess up? So Greenbaum comes to a different kind of end than a lot of mobsters do. Gus Greenbaum also has the distinction of being the only mobster I know of to be called mayor in Las Vegas, or at least the area. There are a couple of unincorporated townships as they're called, and the strip is literally in Paradise.

American Mafia: *Paradise?*

Michael Green: *It's not in Las Vegas, it's Paradise Township, and the casino owners wanted that because they did not want the city to annex them and charge them more in terms of municipal taxes, fees and that sort of thing. And they set up a town board, and Greenbaum was known as the mayor of Paradise and apparently allegedly even gave an inaugural address. The irony of Gus Greenbaum actually being called mayor is that most said way at one point apparently wanted to run for the city commission. And supposedly, Siegel said to him, "We don't run for office. We own the people in office." Well said we wanted respectability. He wanted to be respected as a legitimate businessman, and he was well regarded in Las Vegas as a businessman. Now, his widow went on to be interviewed and talk about various things where there are questions about Sedway's connection to Siegel's murder and other things that were going on. One of the ironies is most Sedway had a nephew, Marvin, who became an optometrist in Las Vegas, was elected to the Legislature and 30 years after his death, still is recalled as this upstanding, dedicated public official. In a sense, Marvin achieved the respectability Moe hoped to get. Moe Sedway also has a bit of a distinction. He testifies before Senator Estes Kefauver's Committee on Organized Crime, and they're asking him about his work, and he starts explaining all of his health problems. And he's saying, 'I had a coronary thrombosis. I've had diarrhea for six weeks, so on and so forth. I don't recommend this life.' Well, it's kind of a reminder. It's not always easy to be a mobster.*

Meyer Lansky in Cuba

Under increasing pressure from Federal prosecutors, Meyer Lansky fled to Cuba where he would set up operations at casinos there with the sanction of Cuban president Fulgencio Batista.

He, along with mobster Lucky Luciano would build an empire in Cuba which flourished until Cuban dictator Fidel Castro took over and nationalized gambling, effectively putting an end to the mob's involvement in Cuba.

By 1960, with the mob's rise on the Strip, state gaming regulators created the notorious List of Excluded Persons, more commonly known as the Black Book of Undesirables banned from casinos, to keep a closer eye on the mob.

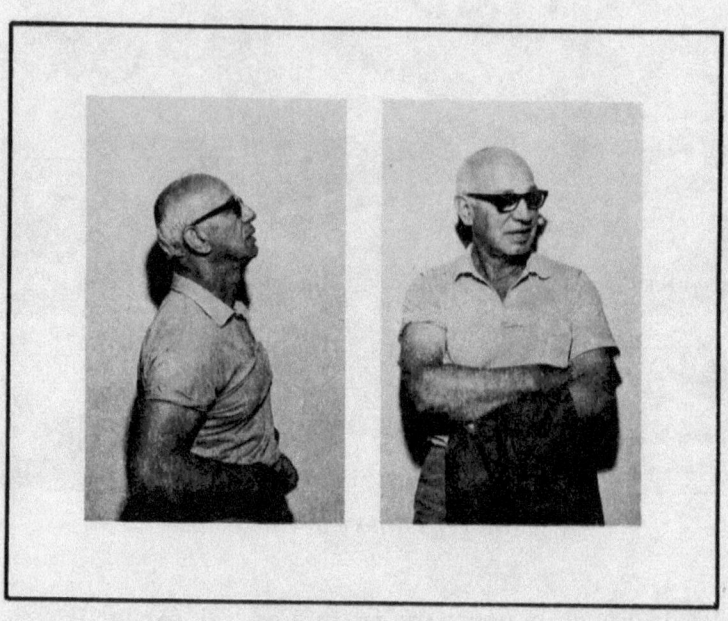

In the first wave of inductees, regulators placed the names of 11 underworld figures, including then-Chicago Mafia boss Sam Giancana and Kansas City crime lords Nick and Carl Civella, into the book.

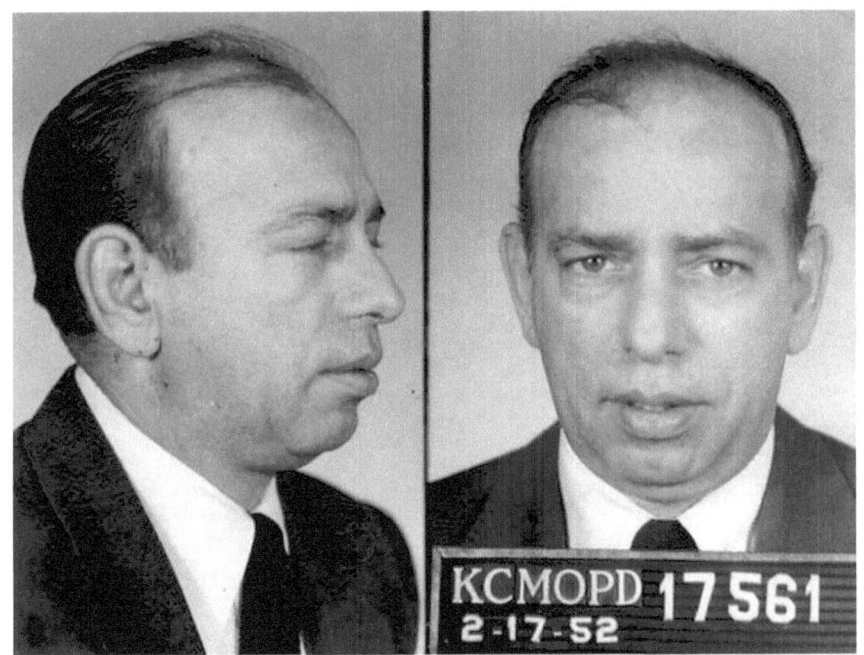
Carl Civella

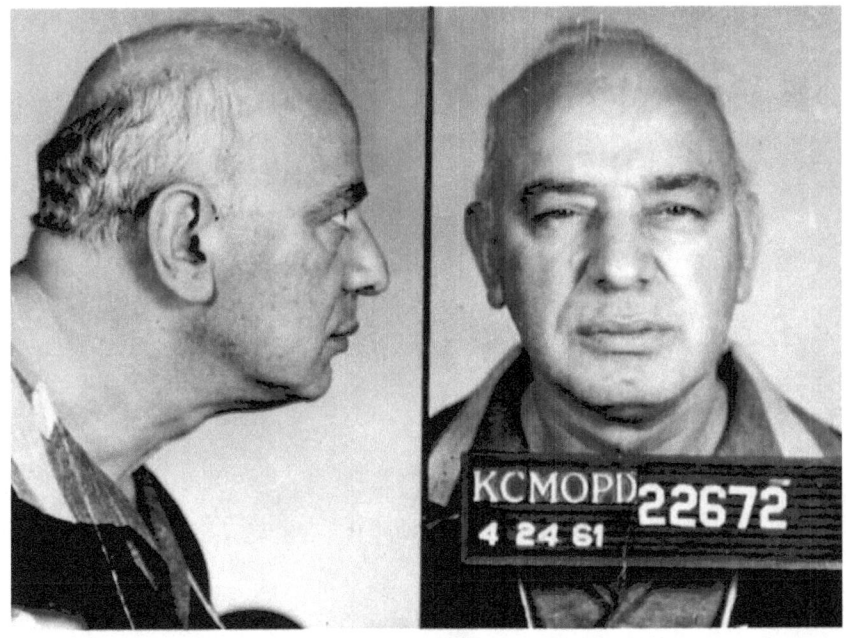
Nick Civella

After President John F. Kennedy was elected, his younger brother Attorney General Robert Kennedy went on a crusade against the mob nationwide and sought to rid Las Vegas casinos of its influence. In senate hearings, Bobby Kennedy famously went after Sam Giancana.

Bobby Kennedy Mob Hearings

Sam Giancana

Up until the mid-1960's the mob had enjoyed almost unlimited growth in Las Vegas. But the dark clouds were growing on the horizon. As Federal authorities and local regulators put the squeeze on the mob, Las Vegas would become the battleground between the forces of good and evil in control of the greatest gambling empire the world had ever known.

Chapter 4:

LAS VEGAS BECOMES AN ENTERTAINMENT MECCA
♠

Throughout the 1960's Las Vegas realized it needed a way to attract the high rollers to the casinos that had sprung up from downtown to the strip. The mob had control of virtually every major hotel in the city and knew it needed a draw. That answer was entertainment.

The showrooms of Las Vegas featured some of the greatest and biggest names in the entertainment and movie industry. This would ensure high rollers from all walks of life would come to Las Vegas for the entertainment and stay at the gaming tables.

Comedians Jimmy Durante, Sophie Tucker, Milton Berle, and Joe E. Lewis, all veterans of nightclubs and vaudeville, were among the first names to grace marquees and helped draw well-dressed crowds that included Hollywood actors and free-spending gamblers.

The Las Vegas strip became the glitzy arena for the likes of Frank Sinatra, Jimmy Durante, Dinah Shore and the Rat Pack. Large scale production shows from Paris gave rise to the iconic Showgirl - which would become the enduring image of Las Vegas.

SHOWGIRL Program for the Lido de Paris at the Stardust Hotel, Las Vegas, circa 1958

*Photograph of Dean Martin and celebrity audience,
Sands Hotel Copa Room, Las Vegas, March 6, 1957*

The very first month of the new decade made entertainment history when the Sands hosted a 3-week "Summit Meeting" in the Copa Room that was presided over by "Chairman of the Board" Frank Sinatra, with Rat Pack cronies Dean Martin, Sammy Davis, Jr., Peter Lawford, and Joey Bishop (all of whom happened to be in town filming Ocean's Eleven).

The series of shows helped to form the Rat Pack legend in Vegas and, in many ways vice versa, making the town hip and cool—the ultimate '60s swinging retreat.

It needed the help. After nearly a decade of almost constant building and expansion (no fewer than 10 major resorts opened in the 1950s), a crackdown on the Mafia and its money, which had fueled the city's development, brought construction to a halt.

Only two major properties opened during the decade—the Road to Morocco–themed Aladdin in 1963 and the Roman Empire bacchanalia that was Caesars Palace in 1966.

Perhaps trying to prove that the mob was gone for good, Las Vegas became a family destination in 1968, when Circus burst onto the scene with the world's largest permanent circus and a "junior casino" featuring dozens of carnival midway games on its mezzanine level.

But at the beginning of the classic lounge act era, which began in the late 1950's and ran well into the end of the 1960's, it was the stars of television and stage which dominated Las Vegas stages.

MICHAEL GREEN

American Mafia: *What kinds of entertainment did Vegas feature in the sixties?*

Michael Green: *The nineteen sixties in Las Vegas in terms of entertainment, were pretty similar to what had come before in the fifties. But what you tended to have in the showrooms would be a headliner and an opening act. So if it's a comedian headliner, then they had a musical opening act and vice versa. But they would also have a line of showgirls. They might have some other acts. Think Vaudeville or the old Ed Sullivan Show. If you're not happy with the singers, the acrobats are coming out in a minute, and at the same time you had these big name entertainers, big singers like Sinatra and Martin, comedians like Johnny Carson coming in and doing these shows, and they tended to be events people looked forward to seeing who was going to come in. There were also great production shows. In nineteen fifty eight, the Stardust opened with the Lido de Paris, so the Tropicana went out and got the folies bergere. Then the dunes got the Casino de Paris, and you had these shows choreographed by a guy named Don Arden, where there was a particular walk that the showgirls were to have. And these shows would usually involve a variety of acts Siegfried and Roy, who later become perhaps the biggest names in Las Vegas entertainment in their time start out at the Tropicana as part of the folies bergere and then are in The Lido. They're one of many acts, something that's worth noting about these shows. The showrooms were not large by today's standards, and shows were to be 90 minutes to two hours because the owners of the casinos wanted people gambling.*

Michael Green: *"The shows were cheap," Frank Sinatra once said. For six bucks, you get filet mignon and me. And then at midnight you had the cocktail show. You had a couple of drinks, and it wasn't that they lost money on the gambling. The question was whether the entertainer brought in gamblers and Sinatra brought in high rollers. He's fine, but Las Vegas would experiment. They would bring in people who you would think would be great entertainers. They didn't bring in the gamblers. They're not invited back there. There's something else going on with entertainment in Las Vegas in the 50s and 60s, and that's the lounge. The Sahara Hotel probably promoted this more than anybody else when they brought in a couple of lounge acts who would be there once the shows were over at eight midnight. Louis Prima with his then wife Keely Smith and his band Sam Butera and the witnesses. And that was just a nightly event and people were singing together, dancing together, and it was just something everybody wanted to see. They also brought in this guy named Don Rickles, who made people laugh by telling them how ugly they were. And somehow it worked. But the lounge was very intimate and you'd also get act. You might expect to be on the strip today, but wouldn't then. The Showboat hotel was a local's place. And for one hundred twenty five a week around nineteen sixty, they had a lounge act named Johnny Cash.*

American Mafia: *Those were really the days of wonderful shows. The golden era of Vegas, many say. So how did the Rat Pack get its start in Vegas?*

Michael Green: *So the Rat Pack consisted of mostly entertainers who regularly performed on the strip Frank Sinatra, Dean Martin, Sammy Davis Jr., Joey Bishop. A good deal at the time. Peter Lawford. Not so much. And what happened was that they were coming to Las Vegas to film Ocean's Eleven, and at about that time, Dwight Eisenhower and Nikita Khrushchev were supposed to have a summit. It didn't come off, but the boss at the Sands, Jack Entratter and his publicist, Al Freeman, hatched this. They called it "The summit at the Sands." The biggest names in entertainment are coming here. They invited Ike and Khrushchev to attend, by the way. They couldn't make it. John Kennedy showed up. He was running for president, and he got some money for his campaign. And he had a good time. But while they were doing Ocean's Eleven, the idea was Who's going to show up? Maybe the Eight pm Show will be Frank and Joey at midnight, Sammy and Peter, and it would just rotate, and instead they'd all give each other a little time to solo. But then they all might be on stage together, and there was a lot of by play, some of it today we would call politically incorrect to the max. But they also were great entertainers who are also, frankly, people of their time. That was part of the appeal. So was the fact that they were, in certain ways, overgrown adolescents doing what they felt like doing? They're up there smoking, drinking, and they're clearly carousing when they're not on stage. Something else that's kind of interesting to think about. You have two sons of Italian immigrants, Sinatra and Martin, an African-American Davis - son of Jewish immigrants, Lawford and an Englishman. Excuse me. You have two Italian people Sinatra and Martin, African-American, Davis, Jewish Bishop, Englishmen, Lawford. In a funny sort of way, this is the melting pot on stage, and it's not that people consciously sat there and said, Oh, I want to watch the combination of people, except that maybe they were great playing off one another. There wasn't in people's minds, I think, social significance, but there may have been to an extent and particularly Frank. Dean and Sammy were major stars in Las Vegas before the Rat Pack, and they would be until the end.*

Casino operators were willing to spend big money to outdo one another by bringing in the biggest names in entertainment.

Marlene Dietrich

Actress Marlene Dietrich received an unprecedented $35,000 a week to perform at the Sahara in 1953, while Liberace's salary seemed to increase with every appearance. He set a record by receiving $50,000 a week to open the Riviera in 1955, and by 1972, he was earning $300,000 a week.

Liberace at His Piano

The Las Vegas Strip had become the most happening place on earth and the opening of new resorts brought even more entertainment luminaries to prominence as showroom stars.

The 1966 opening of Caesars Palace featured singer Andy Williams and the Lennon Sisters, followed by a rotating roster of stars that eventually would include Diana Ross, Cher, Paul Anka, George Burns, Willie Nelson, and Julio Iglesias.

Barbra Streisand - 1966

Little known when she first played Las Vegas, Barbra Streisand was reportedly paid $50,000 to open the International, just off the Strip, in 1969.

Moe Dalitz

But the mob bosses who ran the casinos didn't just stop at the showrooms to attract the high rollers to Vegas.

They were innovative, hosting major golf tournaments and prize fights to attract tourists and money. And they understood business - often investing outside the Strip.

Desert Inn boss Moe Dalitz, formed a development company that built housing tracts, country clubs, and shopping centers.

MOE DALITZ

Morris Moe Dalitz was an American gangster, businessman, casino owner, and philanthropist. He was one of the major figures who shaped Las Vegas in the 20th century. He was often referred to as "Mr. Las Vegas" His investments in Las Vegas began in the late 1940s with the Desert Inn.

Desert Inn Construction

When the original builder of the resort, Wilbur Clark, ran out of money, Dalitz and the Cleveland Mayfield Road Gang bailed him out. The casino opened in 1950. Clark remained the public face and front man of the resort; Dalitz quietly remained in the background as the real owner.

ERIC DEZENHALL

Moe Dalitz was interesting in that he's probably one of the only gangsters who ended up with a legitimate fortune.

People love the mythology that these guys end up with vast amounts of money, and they may in the form of cash. Moe Dalitz, however, was a legal owner of his casinos, primarily the Desert Inn. He also invested very heavily in Las Vegas hospitals, banks, schools, and when he died in 1989, he had a legitimate fortune worth in the hundreds of millions of dollars. He played a similar role to Meyer Lansky, but the basic difference between the two is Moe Dalitz was able to go straight. Meyer was never really able to make that turn because of his association with Lucky Luciano, and he did not die with a large, legitimate fortune. But Moe Dalitz did.

Dalitz also ran the Stardust Resort & Casino for a time after the death of Tony Cornero.

Yet casino owners faced several problems including limited financing. Bankers refused to lend money to casinos, questioning the morality of the business and whether the loans would be repaid. Casinos could rely only on two sources.

The Teamsters Central States Pension Fund was under the control of Allen Dorfman, the adopted son of an Al Capone lieutenant with ties to various organized crime figures.

The Bank of Las Vegas, operated by E. Parry Thomas, represented a group of Utah bankers. Thomas reasoned that Las Vegas casino executives would respond in kind if treated like legitimate businessmen. He was right, but faced criticism that he was a "mob banker."

Allen Dorfman

Allen Melnick Dorfman was a consultant to the International Brotherhood of Teamsters (IBT) Central States Pension Fund. He was a close associate of longtime IBT President.

Jimmy Hoffa was associated with organized crime via the Chicago Outfit. Dorfman was convicted on several felony counts and was murdered in 1983.

Jimmy Hoffa

Jimmy Hoffa became involved with organized crime from the early years of his Teamsters work, a connection that continued until his disappearance in 1975.

He was convicted of jury tampering, attempted bribery, conspiracy, and mail and wire fraud in 1964 in two separate trials. He was imprisoned in 1967 and sentenced to 13 years.

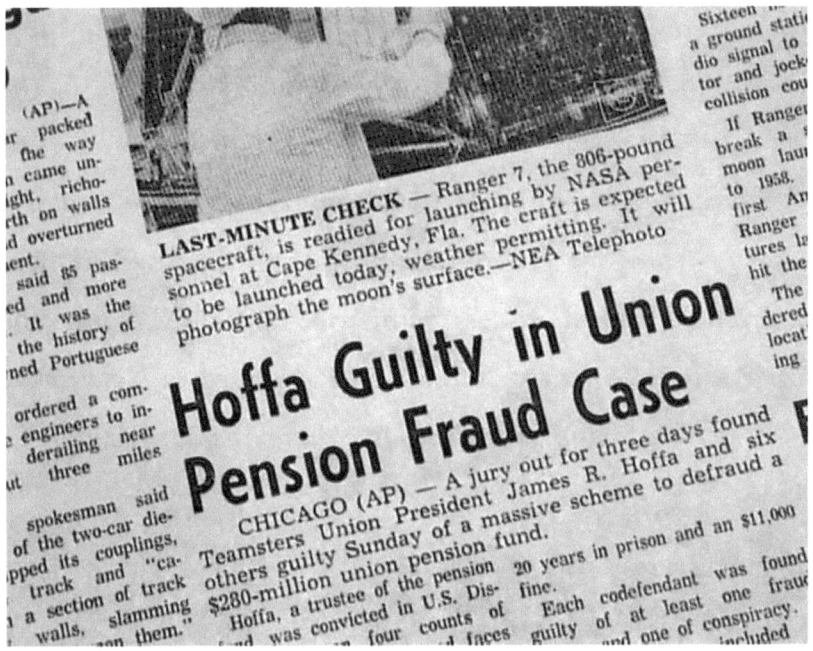

In mid-1971, he resigned as president of the union as part of a commutation agreement with US President Richard Nixon and was released later that year, but Hoffa was barred from union activities until 1980. Hoping to regain support and to return to IBT leadership, he unsuccessfully tried to overturn the order.

Hoffa disappeared on July 30, 1975. He is believed to have been murdered by the Mafia and was declared legally dead in 1982. Hoffa's legacy continues to stir debate.

JEFF BURBANK

Well, Jimmy Hoffa was most certainly killed by the mob, specifically the Detroit outfit along with New Jersey, and the mystery about it is what happened to his corpse. And there have been a lot of diggings, nine different diggings in the Detroit area alone and a lot of outlandish stories. But probably the best story that has the most promise is that a mobster from New Jersey who Hoffa was supposed to meet before he disappeared. His name was Tony Provenzano, the story is that Tony had Jimmy's body shipped to New Jersey and placed into an industrial waste dump inside a barrel.

It's possible Provenzano would use this maybe to have a bargaining chip with the feds if he was nabbed. If he got indicted, maybe could say "Well, I'll tell you where Hoffa's body is, so drop the charges." Or maybe just to have a trophy. Nobody's really sure. Well, we know that barrel was allegedly buried, and it's under some asphalt at a site in New Jersey, and there's a prominent author named Dan Moldea, and he's trying to get the authority to have it dug up.

By the mid-1960s, organized crime figures were growing old. Many had come of age during Prohibition in the 1920s and they were tired of fighting the authorities. State officials wanted to attract more legitimate investors. Federal officials were cracking down on them. Then, Howard Hughes came to town. Nobody knew it yet, but cracks were beginning to appear in the mob's hold on Las Vegas. It was the beginning of the end for mob rule in Sin City.

Chapter 5:

TROUBLE IN PARADISE
♠

Howard Hughes, 1940

From the 1950's into the 1960's it had been a meteoric rise for the mafia in Las Vegas. They had transformed a remote desert town into a thriving mecca for gambling, prostitution and booze -

so much so the metropolis earned an infamous nickname and became known as Sin City. But there was trouble in paradise. As the feds and local regulators cracked down on organized crime, a new face appeared on the desert horizon that would change everything. The man's name was Howard Hughes.

Howard Hughes

Howard Hughes had become one of the world's richest men. His holdings in real estate, movies and a vast empire of diversified investments had afforded him the luxuries of excess.

As a younger man, he'd become a dashing playboy in Hollywood - wooing starlets and playing the role as a debonair and inventive aviator. But over the years his behavior grew erratic and mental health issues plagued him.

Injuries from numerous aircraft crashes caused Hughes to spend much of his later life in pain, and he eventually became addicted to codeine. He'd grown reclusive and eccentric, moving from hotel to hotel, always occupying the upper floors and living in them for extended periods.

Hughes's came to town on November 24, 1966 (Thanksgiving Day). Hughes arrived in Las Vegas by railroad car and moved into the Desert Inn. Because he refused to leave the hotel and to avoid further conflicts with the owners, Hughes bought the Desert Inn in early 1967.

Desert Inn

The hotel's eighth floor became the nerve center of Hughes' empire and the ninth-floor penthouse became his personal residence. Between 1966 and 1968, he bought several other hotel-casinos, including the

Castaways, New Frontier, the Landmark Hotel and Casino, and the Sands.

He bought the small Silver Slipper casino for the sole purpose of moving its trademark neon silver slipper; visible from Hughes' bedroom, as it had apparently kept him awake at night.

Under increasing pressure from local and Federal authorities, the mob had decided to sell its holdings in their Las Vegas hotels to Hughes, opening the door for corporate business interests to take over the ownership and management of these institutions and thus began a cleanup of the grift and corruption that had permeated Las Vegas for over two decades.

Hughes' purchasing Las Vegas casinos ended hidden ownership by organized crime members (such as Dalitz) in Strip casinos. His involvement changed the nation's perception about the gambling business in Las Vegas. This new respectability encouraged public corporations to buy or invest in Nevada casinos as never before. Eventually Hughes would sell his interests to Mormon investment groups, but the die was cast. Legitimacy had finally come to Vegas. But there were still unsavory elements at work as a violent new generation of Mafia upstarts tried milking what was left of the Vegas cow.

The Argent Corporation was a company in Las Vegas that at one time controlled the Hacienda (resort) Hotel/Casino, the Stardust Resort & Casino, the Fremont Hotel and Casino and the casino in the Marina Hotel. The company was owned by Allen Glick, a young attorney and real estate investor from San Diego.

ALLEN GLICK

Glick obtained a $62.7 million loan from the Teamsters through Alan Dorfmann to buy The Stardust and later claimed not to know that he answered to the Chicago, Kansas City, and Milwaukee mobs.

Frank 'Lefty' Rosenthal

If he didn't know, he soon found out when mob bosses installed Frank Rosenthal as their top executive at the two hotels. Rosenthal and his friends apparently devised a successful skimming operation that continued even after state gaming regulators forced them out and new owners took over.

MICHAEL GREEN

Allen Glick's biggest mistake might have been investing in Las Vegas in the first place. He first came into Las Vegas with some partners and bought the Hotel Casino at the far end of the Strip the Hacienda. Then he got a Teamsters loan of more than sixty two million and bought the Stardust and Fremont and was involved in building the Marina. And along the way, he had actually gone to college or something with the son of the head of the Milwaukee mob, Frank Balistrieri. But somewhere in there, Glick was told to hire Frank Rosenthal and did and made the discovery. He said that actually he was working for Rosenthal, not vice versa, and Rosenthal made that very clear to him. Well, ultimately, Rosenthal is brought up for a gambling license. He can't get it. He's forced out. Investigations are going on that show that the Stardust and the other properties were involved in skimming, and Glick eventually has to sell and eventually testifies about what he knew. Well, how much he knew and how much he told have been debated. There was a woman from whom he borrowed money, Tamara Rand, who was in the San Diego area, an investor there, and she was killed. And allegedly the mob did it to get her off Glick's back because she might have been able to tell them about some things. There were questions about Glick's connection to it. And the answer is Glick told his story, and we don't have any really different version to prove otherwise.

LEFTY ROSENTHAL

Frank 'Lefty' Rosenthal with Siegfried and Roy

"Lefty" Rosenthal, was an American professional sports bettor, former Las Vegas casino executive, and organized crime associate.

Rosenthal, who was once called "the greatest living expert on sports gambling" by Sports Illustrated, is credited with bringing sports betting to Las Vegas in the '70s.

Rosenthal's life and career in Las Vegas served as the basis of Martin Scorsese's 1995 film Casino, where he was portrayed by Robert De Niro and re-named Sam "Ace" Rothstein.

In 1976, the FBI and Las Vegas Metropolitan Police Department (LVMPD) discovered that Rosenthal was secretly running four large casinos without obtaining a state gaming license, holding a hearing to determine his legal ability to obtain a license.

The hearing was headed by Nevada Gaming Control Board Chairman (and future U.S. Senator) Harry Reid. Rosenthal was denied a license because of his arrest record, and his documented reputation as an organized crime associate because of his association Chicago mob enforcer Anthony Spilotro.

Frank Balistrieri

On October 4, 1982, Rosenthal survived an assassination attempt in Las Vegas, in which a bomb attached to the gasoline tank was detonated when he started his car. Although never proven, most agreed Milwaukee mob boss Frank Balistrieri was responsible.

Balistrieri, who was known as the "Mad Bomber" to law enforcement, was heard (via wiretap) blaming Rosenthal for the legal problems the mob-controlled casinos were suffering. Similarly, just weeks before the bombing, Balistrieri told his sons he intended to get "full satisfaction" for Rosenthal's perceived wrongdoing.

Ex-Casino Figure Injured As Bomb Explodes In Car

LAS VEGAS, Nev. (UPI) - Frank "Lefty" Rosenthal, ousted by Nevada gaming officials several years ago as head of financier Allen Glick's casino empire, was injured Monday night when a bomb exploded in his car.

Rosenthal, 53, head of the Nevada operations for Glick's now defunct Argent Corporation before both men were forced out of Nevada gambling, suffered burns on both legs and the left side of his face.

A spokesman at Sunrise Hospital said Rosenthal was stable and might be released after being treated.

The explosion occurred about 8:30 p.m. PDT in the parking lot of Marie Callendars restaurant, a family oriented cafe a mile east of the Las Vegas Strip.

"It sounded like a train fell on my roof," said Barbara Lowry, who lives near the restaurant. "His car shot up into the air and flames went two stories high."

Restaurant cashier Lori Wardle said the blast "blew the windows out of the back of the restaurant ... It was a huge explosion."

Mercy Ambulance transported Rosenthal to the hospital along with two other people injured by flying debris.

Portions of Rosenthal's car were spread over a 100-yard area. The bumper of the 1981 Cadillac was 30 yards from where the vehicle had been parked and the trunk was blown 60 yards away.

Homicide and police officers from the Intelligence Division were called to the scene. One policeman said the bomb was either under the car or behind the front seat.

Investigators said an eyewitness told police Rosenthal, dressed in a jogging suit, had just opened the front car door when the bomb went off.

Frank Rosenthal ... hospitalized

Other likely suspects include Kansas City mob bosses, who were recorded on an FBI wiretap tape calling Rosenthal "crazy". Tony the Ant Spilotro was a suspect, either acting with others or on behalf of the Outfit; and outlaw bikers who were friends of Rosenthal's ex-wife, Geri McGee.

Either way, the mob saw Rosenthal as a problem, and when that happens people end up dead. Rosenthal left Las Vegas about six months later, never to return.

JEFF BURBANK

Lefty Rosenthal was this crazy like a fox, brilliant odds maker and Bookmaker from Chicago, And he knew Tony Spilotro really well from their Chicago days, And Rosenthal tried to bribe a couple players into throwing a basketball game and he went to Miami. He was involved in some bombings there. He finally came to Vegas in the 70s and set up a bookmaking operation. And he met up with Tony Spilotro, and they were involved in the skimming that was going on at the Stardust casino. Frank Rosenthal really advanced sports betting like no other person. When he revamped the Stardust Casinos race and sports book, everybody went there.

He had closed circuit TVs, a lot of what was considered state of the art back then. He invented a lot of different things to go with promoting sports betting in casinos that are now part of casinos in Las Vegas today. He was getting too much attention and was on the outs with the mob, especially with Frank Balistrieri out of Milwaukee, and they didn't like how he was operating. He was generating a lot of 'heat' by calling attention to himself. He even had a local TV show and was bringing people on like Sinatra and the bosses were uptight about it.

So someone placed a bomb under his car when he went to a barbecue restaurant in Las Vegas. Someone actually saw someone go under his car and put something there. They didn't know what it was and the bomb exploded. But luckily for Rosenthal, the bottom of that particular car model had a metal plate put in to stabilize it, and that absorbed most of the shock of the bomb. So he survived.

He shouldn't have survived. It should have been more than enough to kill him. But after that, he decided to leave town. He moved to Florida. Well, he knew a lot of things and when you know a lot of things you can end up dead. There were all these fears about so many people by the mob, like, is this person's going to going to flip and provide information that's going to evict us, so we have to kill them first. And that was one of the people that they feared also was really on the outs with Tony Spilotro. And so you can't rule Spilotro out as a suspect in that bombing.

With the takeover of legitimate corporations to manage its gambling palaces and an ever vigilant local council to regulate the gaming industry, Las Vegas was poised for a new era of growth. The mob was on the run and the cleanup had begun. But there would be one last gasp of life from the mafia before the FBI would close in.

Chapter 6:

THE FBI CLOSES IN: CONVICTIONS
♠

Not until the 1970s and 1980s did the mob extend its power and profits beyond the Strip. The Las Vegas gaming commission, along with a relentless FBI task force had largely succeeded in pressuring the mob out of Vegas, conceding its hotels and gambling interests to legitimate corporations. Before the final nail was driven into the coffin for the American Mafia in Las Vegas, another new face appeared in town. His name was Anthony Spilotro.

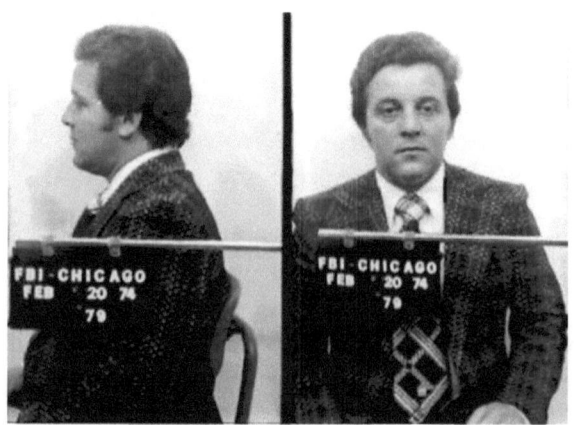

Anthony Spilotro - Mug Shot

Anthony Spilotro, nicknamed Tony the Ant, was an American mobster for the Chicago Outfit who came to Las Vegas in 1971 to run a gift shop at Circus Circus. Spilotro managed the Outfit's illegal casino profits (the "skim") when four of the casinos, The Stardust, The Fremont, The Hacienda, and The Marina, were managed by Frank Rosenthal.

Tony and four of his brothers, (John, Vincent, Victor, and Michael) became involved in criminal activity starting at an early age. The remaining brother, "Patrick" Pasquale Jr., became a dentist.

Frank Cullotta

Spilotro was a boyhood friend of Frank Cullotta, and started a criminal career together as teenagers, engaging in theft, burglary, and murder.

He was nicknamed "Tony the Ant" by the media after FBI Special Agent William Roemer referred to Spilotro as "that little pissant." Since the media couldn't use "pissant", they shortened it to the "Ant".

Spilotro was the leader of the "Hole in the Wall Gang" which he formed in Las Vegas when he moved there in 1971.

The "Hole in the Wall" Gang, was a group of experienced thieves, safecrackers and killers. The crew became known in the media as the "Hole in the Wall Gang" because of its penchant for gaining entry to homes and buildings by drilling through the exterior walls and ceilings of the locations they burglarized.

In early 1979, Frank Cullotta moved to Las Vegas to join Spilotro.

LARRY HENRY:
Broadcast Journalist and Mafia Expert

Las Vegas was an open town for the mob. Various cities had control of different casinos. The Chicago outfit would over time send people to Las Vegas to oversee their entries Johnny Roselli and others. One of the ones they had in Las Vegas from Chicago was a person named Tony Spilotro. He was to oversee the street rackets in Las Vegas. He got there in nineteen seventy one to oversee the scam, which was really being controlled by Lefty Rosenthal inside the Stardust for Argent Corp.. Spilotro was considered a really aggressive person. He was sort of high profile. He made the made the news a lot. And so that created problems for organized crime the same way it did with Frank Rosenthal being high profile. The crime families in the Midwest were concerned about how high profile Spilotro and Rosenthal were. So Spilotro over time became something to too high profile. Over time, there were some incidents that led to him getting into trouble, some legal trouble. Then in nineteen eighty six, he and his brother Michael were taken to a home in suburban Chicago and beaten to death.

They were buried in an Indiana cornfield. It had reached that point with the Midwestern mob, many of whom had just been imprisoned in big trials that they'd had enough with how high profile some of these people were in Las Vegas. It was killing the golden goose. For them, these guys were putting too much heat on them with publicity.

American Mafia: *Why was Frank Cullotta under so much scrutiny by law enforcement?*

Larry Henry: *Frank Cullotta came to Las Vegas at Spilotro's request to help Spilotro run his street operations. They met* the Golden State restaurant - still in Las Vegas on Sahara - to give Cullotta his marching orders. Cullotta oversaw a street rackets gang called the Hole in the Wall Gang. They would knock a hole in the wall of places they would rob. That's why they were called the Hole in the Wall Gang. And then in the early nineteen eighties, they were busted trying to break into a jewelry store on Sahara, near where later Frank Rosenthal's car would blow up.

After he was arrested, Cullotta was told by Federal agents that his life was in danger that Tony Spilotro was going to have him killed. So Cullotta turned on Tony Spilotro. He became a witness for the Federal government. That's one of the things too that led to Spilotro's undoing. Another thing that led to Spilotro's undoing was having a relationship with Frank Rosenthal's wife, Geri. So those things kind of became the perfect storm of problems for the Midwestern mob with the crew they had in Las Vegas when Cullotta turned on Spilotro.

A lot of the House of Cards began to crumble because then he testified in court about some of the things that happened in Las Vegas. In the movie casino, all of this is played out with actors now who are real well known as the characters from the Las Vegas era that's represented in the Spilotro *and Rosenthal escapade. Joe Pesci played a character based on Tony Spilotro, Robert De Niro was the lefty Rosenthal character, and Sharon Stone was the Geri Rosenthal character based on a book by Nicholas Pileggi. So today the public knows a lot about these people, but at that time in Las Vegas, they were pretty unknown. But they were under law enforcement scrutiny. But as Dan Moldea, the great organized crime writer, said, if you're going to have organized crime, you have to have corruption. At some level, I'm paraphrasing. So at that point, there's a lot of suspicion.*

Cullotta testified against Spilotro, and went on to enter the Witness Protection Program and then got out and became a little bit of a mob celebrity. He conducted tours in Las Vegas. He was an advisor for the movie Casino and got paid to be an adviser for the movie. He also appeared in the movie as a hit man, ironically enough, since he actually was a hit man. He had killed some people, including somebody in Las Vegas, on behalf of Spilotro. So that was of significance, and he kept the mob story alive in Las Vegas. He had a YouTube show, and so after the movie Casino in Nineteen Ninety Five, especially after the movie, there's always been interested in the mob. But after that, it really sort of sparked interest in what happened in Las Vegas.

Cullotta kept a lot of that alive over time. He just died about a year ago of COVID 19, in his 80s. Cullotta is dead now, there aren't many people left from that era. One of the last mobsters from that era was somebody named Herbie Blitzstein, they called him Fat Herbie. He was an associate of Spilotro. He was killed. Executed. The last big mob execution in Las Vegas in the mid to late '90s. So all that era kind of came down in the nineties and that that put an end to that whole Casino movie era that most people are familiar with.

Bertha's Gifts & Home Furnishings

On July 4, 1981, the Hole in the Wall Gang robbed Bertha's Gifts & Home Furnishings on East Sahara Avenue in Las Vegas.

Hole In The Wall Gang - Bertha's Burglars - July 4, 1981

The robbery was a bust as much of the gang was arrested, including Cullotta, Joe Blasko, Leo Guardino, Ernest Davino, Lawrence Neumann and Wayne Matecki. Each man was charged with burglary, conspiracy to commit burglary, attempted grand larceny and possession of burglary tools.

Geri McGee - Sharon Stone

Around this time, Spilotro had an affair with Frank Rosenthal's wife. Her name was Geri McGee, with details of the affair fictionalized in the movie 'Casino' directed by Martin Scorcese.

State regulators soon listed him in the Black Book, thanks to allegations that he had been involved in perhaps twenty murders. The gang was apprehended by law enforcement when they were caught during a daring robbery.

Cullotta Arrested

Federal prosecutors obtained several convictions, and induced one Cullotta to testify and enter witness protection.

In 1982, Frank Cullotta was imprisoned. He was approached by the FBI with a wiretap of Spilotro talking with someone about "having to clean our dirty laundry", which Cullotta took as an insinuated contract on his life. Due to this, in July 1982, Cullotta finalized an agreement with the prosecutors.

In September 1983, Spilotro was indicted for conspiracy and obstruction of justice in the Sherwin "Jerry" Lisner murder and released on $100,000 bail.

Cullotta Convicted

At a trial in October 1983, Cullotta admitted that he was involved in over 300 crimes, including four murders, perjury, robberies and burglaries. He also testified that Spilotro, his boss in Las Vegas, ordered him to make a telephone call that lured one of the 1962 murder victims, William McCarthy, to a fast food restaurant.

From then on Cullotta would be known as a 'Rat' for breaking Omerta, the mafia code of silence.

In 1962, Cullotta had killed William McCarthy and James Miraglia, who were found dead in the trunk of a car on May 14, 1962. McCarthy's head had been placed in a vise and his throat slashed, while Miraglia strangled. Spilotro was acquitted later that year. Spilotro's defense attorney was future Las Vegas mayor Oscar Goodman.

William McCarthy and James Miraglia

Oscar Goodman

Oscar Goodman and Anthony Spilotro

During his career as a defense attorney Goodman represented defendants accused of being some of the leading organized crime figures in Las Vegas, such as Meyer Lansky, Nicky Scarfo, Herbert "Fat Herbie" Blitzstein, Phil Leonetti, former Stardust Casino boss Frank "Lefty" Rosenthal, and Jamiel "Jimmy" Chagra, a 1970s drug trafficker who was acquitted of ordering the murder of Federal Judge John H. Wood, Jr.

One of Goodman's notorious clients was reputed Chicago mobster Anthony "Tony the Ant" Spilotro, who was known to have a short and violent temper.

Oscar Goodman and Anthony Spilotro

Joe Pesci in the movie 'Casino'

In the semi-factual 1995 movie Casino, the character of Nicky Santoro was based on Spilotro and was portrayed by actor Joe Pesci.

Oscar Goodman Cameo - 'Casino'

Goodman had a cameo appearance in the film as himself while defending "Ace Rothstein", a character closely based on Lefty Rosenthal and played by Robert De Niro.

MICHAEL GREEN

If I had to list the most fascinating characters in the history of Las Vegas, Oscar Goodman is going to be high on the list. He's a well-trained attorney, comes from a good family. He comes out to Las Vegas with his new young wife, Carolyn. They fall in love with the place, ultimately. And he ends up representing organized crime figures now. At the time he started in the mid 60s, defense work was not necessarily the kind of specialty it became or that profitable necessarily. Lawyers tended to be generalists. There were a few big, prominent defense attorneys, yes, but Oscar Goodman is an example. He represented Rosenthal not only in terms of illegal activities that he was defending him, but for his gaming licensing. He could do all these things. Well, Goodman, when I was growing up, was on TV. Every day you saw him going to and from court with somebody. He was being interviewed and he's incredibly articulate. He's blunt. I've claimed for years and I was wrong, frankly, that there was no filtration system between his brain and his mouth. No, if you are a really good defense attorney. And believe me, if I was in trouble, I'd want him to represent me. But there actually is a filter. You know what you're doing and saying. And at the same time, that seeming lack of a filtration system helped get him elected. He was the anti-politician politician. He'd never run for office before. And he was blunt and open. What also helped him, truthfully, is a tendency among some Las Vegans to wish for a time that never really existed, that the mob ran everything and things were so much cheaper and the streets were safe. Well, the streets weren't entirely safe, proof of which is the mob was involved in crime. Were things cheaper considering inflation? Yes. But were they better? We can always debate those kinds of things. But there was this nostalgia for the older Las Vegas that I think Oscar Goodman embodied, and as it turned out, he was a wildly popular three term mayor and a very successful one. And that included a lot that changed the vibe, appearance and success of downtown Las Vegas and the surrounding area. Yeah, he was controversial. He's going to say things that get you mad. But Oscar Goodman loves Las Vegas. And I think that is also what he conveyed to voters.

Goodman currently owns and operates a steakhouse in Las Vegas, and is a well-respected figure in the city.

Oscar Goodman

'Being Oscar' Book Cover

He also authored a book, "Being Oscar: From Mob Lawyer to Mayor of Las Vegas." If truth could be said to be more ironic than fiction, Oscar Goodman's story would serve as the prime example.

The Federal crackdown on the mob and the indictments that followed for key members of the organization and its associates would be the final death blow. What is generally considered the "Mob Era" of Las Vegas ended in the mid-1980s with the death or imprisonment of many key players and a corporate culture emerging on the Strip and downtown.

LARRY HENRY

American Mafia: *How did corporate ownership change Las Vegas?*

Larry Henry: *When the mob came in, in the mid-forties and really got their foothold in Las Vegas, they were sort of sort of on their own. A lot of mobsters who were bootleggers and mobsters back East as well as the Midwest came to Las Vegas because gambling and bookmaking was legal. Over time, several things happened that cut away at their power in Las Vegas. One was the Black Book that started in 1960, and they still have it. It's a book that gaming regulators have created that is a list of people who are allowed in* casinos. The first black book, some of the first versions of it, had people like Sam Giancanna from Chicago mob boss and Chicago Nick Civella, mob boss in Kansas City. Spilotro ended up in it. Rosenthal ended up in it, so the Black Book had a big part in highlighting who people were that were mobsters in Las Vegas. Another big factor was the 1969 Corporate Gaming Act which allowed casinos to be owned by corporations so that each individual in the corporation didn't have to be licensed. In the past, everybody involved had to be licensed. A lot of mobsters had secret ownership of casinos and weren't licensed. They were getting a percentage of the profits illegally. But those who are who are who or who are considered owners of the casino had to be licensed.

American Mafia: *So the mob guys were being forced out by regulations designed to drain the swamp.*

Larry Henry: *In a manner of speaking, yes. Corporations began to take over casinos, and those are publicly traded and owned by shareholders. Everybody who owns shares in a corporation, whether it's Wal-Mart, McDonald's or Ballys, they have weight. Same with the corporations that owned casinos. It puts control in the hands of big business run in a sense by average citizens. So the corporations began to get control of Las Vegas casinos and that changed the tenor of Las Vegas.*

Another thing that really changed it, too, was the RICO Act. There was a Federal statute that allowed mob organizations to be to be pursued legally from the hierarchy down. You could go after the organization, not just individuals. Some of the top people in mob organizations protected themselves by having underlings get their hands dirty. Those are the ones who were in prison, but the RICO statute in allowed organizations to be pursued. So those things really began to stack up: the black book, corporate ownership of casinos and RICO. Those things began to allow inroads into knocking out the mob. Plus, the Federal government began to put strike task force in in cities like Las Vegas. They were very aggressive in going after the mob. Bobby Kennedy when he was attorney general in the early sixties, a lot of effort was put behind his campaign on knocking out the mob.

Chapter 7:

THE MAFIA IN LAS VEGAS ENDS
♠

With the mob's control nearly ended, the mid-1980's began a new era for Las Vegas. The men who now ran the town were no longer the Godfathers, but new civic minded leaders that had a grand vision for their city of gold. Plans were underway to make Las Vegas a family attraction. But just as that was happening, the last vestige of mob control came to a violent end in an Indiana cornfield for one of Las Vega's more notorious actors, that of Anthony 'THE ANT' Spilotro.

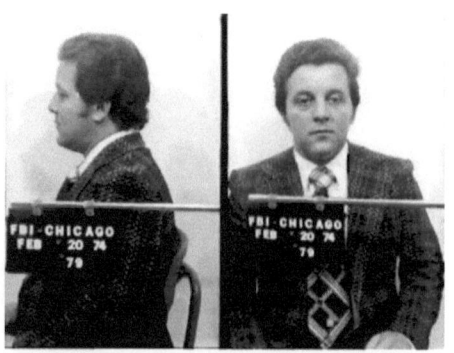

Anthony Spilotro - Mug Shot

Tony and Michael Spilotro

Tony Spilotro faced numerous indictments by 1986, when he and his brother Michael traveled to Chicago in hopes of taking over the Chicago mob after the conviction of several of the old dons.

Instead, their campaign failed, they disappeared, and they turned up dead.

Spilotro Brothers grave

Nine days later they we found buried in an Indiana cornfield, near a farm owned by one of the convicted Chicago leaders.

It is suspected that Spilotro and his brother Michael were called by "Black Sam" Carlisi to a meeting at a hunting lodge owned by Spilotro's former mob boss, Joseph Aiuppa. Original reports stated the Spilotro's were savagely beaten and buried alive in a cornfield in Enos, Indiana. They were identified by their brother Pasquale, Jr. through dental x-ray records.

Joseph Aiuppa

MICHAEL GREEN

American Mafia: *Why were Tony Spilotro and his brother murdered?*

Michael Green: *Kind of depends on who's telling the story, perhaps. Eventually there was a trial. They called it the 'family secrets case' where they talked about who did it and why. Certainly, there was a fight going on over who would control the Chicago mob, and the fight originated in part because the Federal government was able to get convictions of the leaders. And a lot of that story was tied to Las Vegas, and Spilotro was supposed to be controlling things in Las Vegas. So how much of it was Spilotro, in essence, running for leadership? How much of it was him being blamed for the fact that now you had a vacuum or at least a competition for leadership? And I think those things enter into it. I don't think it's a thought that he's going to talk. I don't think Tony Spilotro ever would have talked. But clearly, there were some things going on within the mob that had an impact on ultimately his death.*

American Mafia: *Why did they murder his brother as well?*

Michael Green: *I would say part of the issue with his brother is that he was part of the family, which I use in a couple of ways, but certainly Spilotro, his family and his own connections, his own loyalties were involved. And there's evidence to suggest that Tony was trying to protect Michael at the end as they were being killed. Now you've got the rest of the family. They had a brother who was a dentist. He wasn't a mobster. He was a dentist. But Michael was closer to the action, and that probably had a lot to do with it.*

GARY JENKINS

Why were Tony Spilotro and his brother Michael murdered? I would say, if you're going to kill one brother, you better kill all the brothers and Tony and Michael Spilotro were in business together in the gold rush that was Las Vegas at the time. They were both running the Hole in the Wall Gang and they were, you know, partners in crime as well as brothers and blood in the mob. The outfit in Vegas and the outfit in Chicago wanted to kill Tony Spilotro. I think they needed to send a message to everybody else. They felt like it was his fault things were falling apart. He was to blame that the whole thing fell down in Las Vegas with the FBI. The FBI made all these cases on all the mob bosses in Chicago, Joey Aiuppa, Jackie Sharon, Angela Pietra. Kansas City, Milwaukee and Cleveland all felt like it was Tony Spilotro drawing so much heat and he didn't keep Lefty Rosenthal under control like he was supposed to. He had this burglary gang going, [The Hole In the Wall Gang] and they all fell and he was going to catch a case behind that. It looked like Frank Cullotta was going to turn and testify against Spilotro. So he had a lot of heat on him and more than likely he had not been kicking back money from this Hole in the

Wall Gang. That's another big no, no with the outfit. If you're one of their guys and you've got a nice piece of action coming in and you don't kick back, at least a taste to them, well that's just like stealing to them. So all those things combined to, you know, we're going to we're just going to have to make an example out of Tony Spilotro and get him out of the picture.

In 2007, mob assassin Nicholas Calabrese testified at the "Operation Family Secrets" trial in Chicago that the Spilotro brothers were killed in a Bensenville, Illinois basement where the Spilotros believed Michael would be inducted into The Outfit.

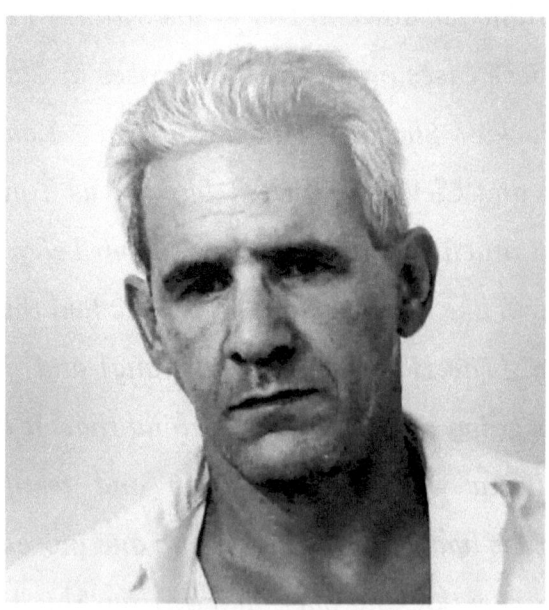

Nicholas Calabrese

According to court testimony, when Tony entered the basement and realized what was about to occur, he asked if he could "say a prayer".

By the time of the Spilotro murders, Federal authorities had convicted a string of Midwest Mafia bosses for skimming money at the Stardust, Fremont and Tropicana casinos. Other mob figures had been convicted in Detroit and Las Vegas of wielding hidden influence at the Aladdin.

The mob had lost its grip on the Strip, and its control over street rackets diminished.

Steve Wynn

Enter the man who change the face of Las Vegas forever – Steve Wynn. Wynn's first major casino on the Las Vegas Strip was The Mirage, which opened on November 22, 1989. It was the first time Wynn was involved with the design and construction of a casino.

The Mirage

He financed the $630 million project largely with high-yield bonds issued by Michael Milken. Its construction is also considered noteworthy in that The Mirage was the first casino to use security cameras full-time on all table games.

LARRY HENRY

American Mafia: *How did Las Vegas become Disneyland for families and why did this change?*

Larry Henry: *In 1989, a casino developer named Steve Wynn, who had owned the Golden Nugget in downtown Las Vegas and been involved in different capacities in Las Vegas, built the Mirage. It's still in existence on the west side of the Las Vegas Strip. It was really a big themed resort and the first of the Big Mega resorts. It had a theme to it. It attracted families, and that kicked off a trend in Las Vegas of Big Mega Resorts, The Excalibur, Big New York, New York, the Luxor... big casinos that had rides and family attractions. Treasure Island with pirate ships. There was a volcano in front of the mirage. All those sort of things made it kind of a Disney-like atmosphere.*

American Mafia: *So the mob was forced to leave town and then the business model changed?*

Larry Henry: *Yes, with less emphasis on gaming. By 1999 Las Vegas casinos began to make more money off of conventions, hotel amenities like food and entertainment, then gambling. During that period from the period of the Mirage opening to nineteen ninety nine Las Vegas really changed. The economy of scale changed. It used to be a town where gamblers could come in, get a cheap food dollar ninety nine buffet and a cheap hotel room. They wanted you on the gaming floor because the odds favor the casino on casino* games. So by getting you to Las Vegas with cheaper rooms, cheap food, they would get your money at the gaming tables.

That began to change, though, when the mega resorts were built. You're talking about thirty five hundred room hotels. The El Rancho Vegas had sixty three hotel rooms, so suddenly you needed more people spending more money on things besides casino games. So that started the mega resort trend on the strip trend on the Strip with really big hotels, the newest one to open this summer in June called Resorts World Las Vegas. It's thirty five hundred hotel rooms where the Stardust used to be, as The Stardust was imploded. Resorts World was built where [The Stardust] used to be. The Stardust was the hotel that Lefty Rosenthal ran, where Tony Spilotro and the Chicago outfit were involved in the scheme overseeing the skim. So that's how Las Vegas changed. It became a place where money was made, not so much on gambling anymore. Vegas still makes a lot of money on gambling. But all of these conventioneers who come to town, they'll spend a lot of money on high end shopping, like Versace, or Gucci all who have shops in these large megamalls and inside the casinos themselves. It's now the shopping and the restaurants. In the old days, there was sort of a tawdry aspect to Las Vegas. Nude dancers in shows, there was a sexual vibe. One of the casinos even had nudes on ice. That wouldn't happen in Las Vegas today. They're trying to get a crowd now that's more interested in things like high end shopping, high end dining, more luxurious hotels.

That's what Las Vegas is about right now. An example, too of the way Las Vegas has changed because of the way sports wagering is controlled by organized crime. Major sports leagues would not go to Las Vegas, it was looked down upon. NFL, NHL, WNBA those leagues wouldn't have gone to Las Vegas not that long ago, but now the Las Vegas Raiders are in town moved from Oakland. The Vegas Golden Knights from the NHL are in town at T-Mobile on the Las Vegas Strip. The WNBA has a team there. The Oakland A's are looking at it, so that also reflects how Las Vegas has changed.

It wasn't that long ago that a lot of people thought of Las Vegas as sort of a tawdry, mobbed up place. Now it's seen as kind of a high end experience that still has a lot of that. It still has the gambling and things like that. But that also is what draws interest to people who want to learn about the mob in Las Vegas.

The Mob Museum is perfect example of that a world class museum that people flock to because they want to see it.

People always ask "Where was the casino that Lefty Rosenthal worked at? Where did Tony Spilotro run his gift shop?" They now want to see all of that. They still ask "Where did Frank Rosenthal's car blow up?" because of movies like Casino... Because of interest in the mob in Las Vegas, which has been sort of pushed aside the mob, people are really interested in learning about it.

American Mafia: *And of course, that is why they want to see our documentary!*

Siegfried and Roy

The hotel became the main venue for the Siegfried & Roy show in 1990, and in 1993 the hotel hosted the Cirque du Soleil show Nouvelle Experience. Wynn's next project, Treasure Island Hotel and Casino, opened in the Mirage's old parking lot on October 27, 1993, at an overall cost of $450 million. The establishment was the home of the first permanent Cirque du Soleil show in Las Vegas.

Fat Herbie Blitzstein

But what was thought to have been the end of the mob in Vegas was to be short lived. Fat Herbie Blitzstein, Tony Spilotros right hand man was released from prison only to return to Vegas in the early 1990s.

Fat Herbie picked where he'd left off. After prison, the 62-year-old Blitzstein set up a downtown auto-repair shop, a front for his loan shark and insurance-fraud racketeering operations.

Fat Herbie

In January 1997, Blitzstein was murdered, shot once in the back of the head in a contract hit and attempt to take over his racketeering business. Federal prosecutors contended during Fat Herbie's murder trial that mob families in Los Angeles and Buffalo, N.Y., had ordered Blitzstein hit so they could take control of his rackets.

JEFF BURBANK

Fat Herbie Blitzstein was another Spilotro crony from Chicago who Tony Spilotro brought in to help him with his criminal conspiracies, and he worked at Spilotro's jewelry store named 'The Gold Rush' and helped with their fencing and various criminal activities after Spilotro died. When Fat Herbie got out of prison on an earlier conviction he came back to Las Vegas and ran some street rackets like loan sharking and he had more than two hundred and fifty thousand dollars on the street, which was pretty good, and he would make money from the interest from American gamblers. He also had a car insurance scam going on in a bike shop that he owned with another person with mob ties. The problem for him was the low level hoods. There were some really smart people running the Las Vegas rackets but then there were some low level, not very bright people from the Buffalo mob and the Los Angeles mob coming in trying to lean on street rackets, and they wanted to take over Blitzstein's street rackets. He wouldn't cooperate, so they hired to hit man to go in and kill him at his home. So he was a shot to death while at home.

By the late 1980's and into the early 90's a great transformation was taking place in Las Vegas. The old hotels were being demolished. Grand new palaces were being funded by corporate investment groups to replace the grift of petty gangsters into a moneymaking juggernaut.

The gun had been replaced by the balance sheet. In the coming decade the era of excess would culminate in a corporate-run empire that would make even the mob sit up and take notice.

But the mob had been sent packing. The American Mafia's hold on the United States was diminishing dramatically and would soon be almost completely eradicated.

Chapter 8:

CORPORATIONS TAKE OVER
♠

Mirage Volcano

By the 1990's the Las Vegas skyline was starting to become transformed. Large construction cranes loomed against the sky, older hotels were being demolished as a new era dawned for the approaching new millennia. As the last vestiges of a bygone era were being imploded and replaced anew, the question of the future of Las Vegas looked promising."

Steve Wynn

On Nov. 22, 1989, Steve Wynn opened the Mirage, the first new casino to be built in 16 years. It ignited a resort building boom that revolutionized Vegas into the 1990s and 2000s.

The Rio, the Luxor, the Excalibur and Treasure Island were soon to follow, offering themed entertainment, lodging and dining experiences that rivaled world class resorts.

But even a savior like Wynn was reputed to have links to organized crime, particularly to Maurice Friedman.

Steve Wynn and Frank Sinatra

Friedman, who lived in Las Vegas, was linked to a branch of the Mafia in Detroit. When Wynn's father died he left Wynn with 350,000 in gambling debts. But he'd also left his bingo parlor to his son, and Steve Wynn took it over.

Using Friedman's contacts and a $30,000 loan from a family friend, Steve Wynn bought three percent of the Frontier Hotel on the Las Vegas Strip in 1965. The total cost of this venture was $45,000.

New Frontier Hotel & Casino

He soon borrowed another $30,000 from a Las Vegas bank to acquire an additional two percent stake in the hotel and casino. This amount of shares allowed Steve to qualify for a small portion of the Frontier's gambling profits.

Steve and Elaine Wynn

In 1967, Steve and his wife Elaine Wynn moved to Las Vegas. He became the Frontier's slot and casino manager. He was only 25-years old, but within a short time, Friedman was implicated in a card cheating scheme in California and his affiliation with the Detroit Mafia came to the surface.

5 Found Guilty in Friars Club Card-Cheating Conspiracy Trial

BY GENE BLAKE
Times Staff Writer

All five defendants in the Friars Club card-cheating conspiracy case were found guilty Monday on all 49 felony counts after a federal court trial of nearly six months.

A jury of 10 women and two men returned the verdicts before U.S. Dist. Judge William P. Gray, culminating about 22 hours of deliberations spread over four days.

Judge Gray set Jan. 20 for sentencing and hearing arguments on motions for acquittal, new trials

Alleged bribery investigated in Friars case. See Page 3, Part 1.

130 years for another, Maurice H. Friedman. Fines of $5,000 on some counts and $10,000 on others also could be imposed.

Benjamin J. Teitelbaum could receive up to 83 years, John Rosselli 43 years and Manuel (Ricky) Jacobs 38 years, along with fines.

A sixth defendant, Dr. Victor G. Lands, pleaded guilty to one count of falsifying an income tax return and did not stand trial. He also will be sentenced Jan. 20.

All five who went to trial were convicted of engaging in a five-year conspiracy to violate federal laws by cheating wealthy members of the exclusive Friars Club in Beverly Hills at gin rummy.

The Frontier's investors quickly sold the hotel-casino to Howard Hughes for $24 million. As a minority investor who was only entitled to gambling profits, Steven Wynn did not see anything significant from the sale.

Howard Hughes - Frontier

Steve Wynn Eyeing the Prize

Wynn continued to borrow and invest in Las Vegas casinos, until he was able to acquire enough shares in the Golden Nugget to become its Chairman.

MICHAEL GREEN

Ultimately, corporate ownership remakes Las Vegas gaming. The state changed its laws in the late 60s. Until that time, every person who had any ownership in a casino had to be licensed, which made it impossible for a publicly traded corporation to own a casino. Well, they changed the law, and corporations were allowed to come in. You don't see the overwhelming presence of corporations until the 90s. Las Vegas in the seventies and eighties isn't a fallow period, but it's a lot slower and they're in the process of getting rid of the mob operators. Well, now they're gone. And what's going to happen? Well, there was a line Steve Wynn had. Las Vegas doesn't need another casino, but it sure could use an attraction. And the opening of the Mirage in November of nineteen eighty nine helps create that attraction. The Excalibur follows the following year, but they were still pretty much locally based people, even if they were involved in some other jurisdictions like Atlantic City and Wall Street hadn't bought in. But it isn't until they're successful. And then Kirk Kerkorian, who had already built a couple of major properties, opens the MGM Grand in ninety three and you're seeing more expansion that corporate America really sees Las Vegas as a great investment today.

Very few corporations own most of the hotels: MGM, Caesars Entertainment, Las Vegas Sands Corp., Wynn. Those are most of the owners of the major strip hotels. The changes reflect the corporations, but also reflect that gambling is now legal in 48 of 50 states in some form. You don't have to come to Nevada to gamble. So what else is being offered? Well, you have foodie destination tourism. The celebrity chefs, shopping pools, nightclubs. You have arenas for the major entertainers. And this does all go ultimately to the major difference corporations make when the mob controlled the casinos. In the mob days the profit was in skimming the money. That's where the money was. So cheap entertainment, good food. But it's cheap, nice rooms today. Luxurious rooms, major entertainment and arenas, major shopping, major food and every department is supposed to be profitable. And that means the bargains that people used to see you're less likely to find. It also means you're likely to see more elaborate entertainment and you're likely to eat much better food.

Steve Wynn, Chairman

Golden Nugget Atlantic City

Steve Wynn expanded his holdings to open another Golden Nugget in Atlantic City, but soon ran afoul with the New Jersey Casino Control Commission. In 1984, the commission had alleged evidence tying Wynn to New York mobster Anthony Salerno.

ANTHONY SALERNO

Anthony "Fat Tony" Salerno (August 15, 1911 – July 27, 1992) was an American mobster who served as underboss and front boss of the Genovese crime family in New York City from 1981 until his conviction in 1986.

Salerno was born and raised in East Harlem, New York. In his youth, he became involved in gambling, numbers, loansharking and protection rackets for the Luciano family, which later came to be known as the Genovese family. Salerno was a member of the 116th Street Crew, headed by Michael "Trigger Mike" Coppola. Salerno climbed the family ranks by controlling a possible million-dollar-a-year numbers racket operation in Harlem and a major loansharking operation. In 1948, Coppola fled to Florida to escape murder charges, and Salerno took over the crew.

In 1959, Salerno was a secret financial backer of a heavyweight professional boxing title fight at New York's Yankee Stadium between Swedish boxer Ingemar Johansson and American boxer Floyd Patterson. No charges were filed against Salerno. Salerno divided his time between a home in Miami Beach, Florida, a 100-acre estate and horse farm in upstate Rhinebeck, New York, the Palma Boys Club in East Harlem, and his apartment in the upscale Gramercy Park section of Manhattan. Salerno served as consigliere, underboss, and acting boss of the Genovese family.

By the 1960s, Salerno controlled the largest numbers racket operation in New York, grossing up to $50 million per year. Salerno kept his headquarters at the Palma Boys Social Club in East Harlem and continued to work in these areas. The FBI accused him of heading a bookie and loan shark network that grossed $1 million annually. Salerno hired Roy Cohn as his attorney. On April 20, 1978, Salerno was sentenced to six months in Federal prison for illegal gambling and tax evasion charges. In early 1981, after his release from prison, Salerno suffered a mild stroke and retreated to his Rhinebeck estate to recuperate. At the time of his stroke, Salerno was Genovese underboss.

After Salerno's recovery from his stroke and the March 31, 1981 death of Genovese front boss Frank Tieri, Salerno succeeded him. Although law enforcement at the time thought that Salerno was the boss of the Genovese family, it was an open secret in New York Mafia circles that Salerno was merely a front man for the real boss, Vincent "the Chin" Gigante. For instance, Alphonse "Little Al" D'Arco, who later became acting boss of the Lucchese crime family before turning informer, told investigators that when he became a Lucchese made man in 1982, he was told that Gigante was the boss of the Genovese family. Ever since the death of boss Vito Genovese in 1969, the real family leader had been Philip "Benny Squint" Lombardo. Over the years, Lombardo used several front bosses to hide his real status from law enforcement, a practice continued when Gigante took over the family upon Lombardo's retirement in 1981.

On February 25, 1985, Salerno and eight other New York bosses on the "Mafia Commission" were indicted in the Mafia Commission Trial. In October 1986, Fortune Magazine named the 75-year-old Salerno as America's top gangster in power, wealth and influence. For that reason, he was nominally the lead defendant in the trial. Many observers disputed Salerno's top ranking, claiming that law enforcement greatly exaggerated Salerno's importance to *bring attention to their legal case against him. Salerno's bail request was denied and his attorneys appealed the decision all the way to the United States Supreme Court. However, in United States v. Salerno the Supreme Court ruled that he could be held without bail because of his potential danger to the community. Along with the other defendants of the trial, Salerno pleaded not guilty on July 1, 1985. On November 19, 1986, Salerno was convicted on RICO charges. On January 13, 1987, he was sentenced, along with six other defendants, to 100 years in prison without parole and fined $240,000.*

While awaiting the Mafia Commission trial, Salerno was indicted in a separate trial on March 21, 1986, in a second Federal racketeering indictment, which accused Salerno of having hidden controlling interests in S & A Concrete Co. and Transit-Mix Concrete Corp. in the construction of Mount Sinai School of Medicine, Memorial Sloan-Kettering Cancer Center, and the Trump Tower. Salerno was also accused of illegally aiding the election of Roy Lee Williams to the national presidency of the Teamsters Union. Salerno pleaded not guilty on all charges. In October 1988, he was convicted and sentenced to 70 years in prison, including a $376,000 fine, and ordered to forfeit half of the racketeering proceeds (estimated to be $30 million).

In 1986, shortly after Salerno's conviction in the Commission Trial, Salerno's longtime right-hand man, Vincent "The Fish" Cafaro, turned informant, and told the FBI that Salerno had never been the real boss of the Genoveses, but was merely a front for Gigante. Cafaro also revealed that the Genovese family had been keeping up this ruse since 1969. An FBI bug had captured a conversation in which Salerno and capo Matthew "Matty the Horse" Ianniello were reviewing a list of prospective candidates to be made in another family. Frustrated that the nicknames of the wannabes hadn't been included, Salerno shrugged and said, "I'll leave this up to the boss"–a clear sign that he was not the real leader of the family. However, according to New York Times organized crime reporter Selwyn Raab, even though prosecutors erred in billing Salerno as the Genovese boss, this mistake would not have jeopardized Salerno's conviction at the Commission Trial or his 100-year sentence. In his book, Five Families, Raab noted that Salerno had been tried and convicted for specific criminal acts, not for being a boss.

After his conviction and imprisonment, Salerno's health deteriorated due to his diabetes and suspected prostate cancer. On July 27, 1992, Anthony Salerno died at the Medical Center for Federal Prisoners in Springfield, Missouri.

Salerno was buried at Saint Raymond's Cemetery in the Throggs Neck section of the Bronx in New York City. Salerno is portrayed by Paul Sorvino in the film Kill the Irishman (2011) and Domenick Lombardozzi in the film The Irishman (2019).

Anthony Salerno

Salerno had by then become America's top gangster in power, wealth and influence. Known as Fat Tony, Salerno was a member of the Vito Genovese La Cosa Nostra organized crime family.

The commission alleged that the mob was laundering money through Wynn's Atlantic City property. The charges were never proven, as there was no direct link between Wynn and the mobsters.

However, the whole charade left a bad taste in Steve's mouth and he sold the Atlantic City casino, making a profit of $260 million for the company.

In the 1990s Wynn conceived of a new kind of Strip mega resort. As the years had gone by, the new resorts modeled after his vision had become more and more Disney-esque and cartoonish. He envisioned something more elegant that hearkened back to the glamorous Rat Pack days of the Strip.

He acquired the downtrodden Dunes Hotel site and had it imploded on live TV in 1993. Five years later the $1.6 billion Bellagio opened. Once again, Wynn had raised the standards for new Strip resorts.

After the Bellagio opened, another building frenzy hit the Strip with competitors desperate to keep up with Wynn. The megaresorts born out of this boom include Paris-Las Vegas and Mandalay Bay.

But unlike the gangsters who had come to Las Vegas and transformed a dusty speck of town in the middle of a barren desert into a neon lit gambling mecca, Wynn had done it the legal way.

ERIC DEZENHALL

One of the things that Meyer Lansky wrote about and talked about privately was how he and his partners were muscled out of the casino business by legitimate corporations. What he meant by that was he could only raise so much money from the mob, whereas in an initial public offering, you could raise untold millions of dollars, which is what legitimate corporations did. What Howard Hughes and other legitimate owners did was they hired former FBI agents as executives, and they then approached mobsters who were reluctant to sell their casinos and basically said, I think you should sell, you know, my friend, Mr. Smith and Mr. Jones, they were former FBI agents and they have a lot of contacts in Washington and the Justice Department, and it would probably be a good idea for you to sell. And contrary to the popular belief of mobsters as these fearless characters, they were terrified of getting prosecuted in their old age, and it was easier to sell out than it was to maintain ownership of the casinos. And this was something that Meyer was very bitter about for the rest of his life that ironically, he and his friends were muscled out of the business they created by legitimate hotel casino owners. The biggest things that hurt organized crime in the 80s and

90s were number one, the RICO law, which allowed broad capability for the government to prosecute people, even if they couldn't necessarily prove individual discrete crimes.

Second, the competent leadership of the mob was dying off and aging, and so you didn't have as smart, talented people. You also had superior surveillance where they were actually able to capture these guys on video and audio and prosecute them. You also had the rise of narcotics and given the prison sentences for narcotics, you had a lot of people who were turning state's evidence and ratting out their superiors. So all of those things came together in the 70's, 80's and 90's to cause really big trouble for the mob. The mob didn't really have serious casino interests in the 2000s. By that time, they had been run out to the extent they had a presence at all. It was probably at the tail end of the unions, maybe they still had local street crime. But given that casino corporations had to literally sign away their civil rights to be executives that did not allow for mob infiltration. By the 2000s, the mob, for all intents and purposes, was really out of Las Vegas. There was nothing left for them in the casinos.

As the building boom exploded and the expansion of Las Vegas continued at a dizzying pace, the intent was clear for its future to adopt a family friendly atmosphere. City leaders wanted to make Sin, Sex and Gambling, its main source of profits, into a family affair.

Chapter 9:

LAS VEGAS BECOMES DISNEYLAND
♠

Las Vegas Nevada. What was once a mecca for sin was now reframed as a Disneyland for adults who could also bring their families.

Disney – Las Vegas

Themed hotels featured programmed experiences designed to appeal to the whole family.

Gone were the days of strip joints and rampant prostitution, but it was never that far away for those who desired it. But as Steve Wynn continued to expand his empire of themed hotels, some speculated the mob's influence might still have its tentacles in the profits.

OSCAR GOODMAN

In 1999 mob attorney turned Mayor Oscar Goodman, a former criminal defense attorney and self-described mouthpiece for the mob denied the mob's existence in Las Vegas. He'd spent 35 years defending the nation's most notorious underworld figures. Besides Spilotro, Goodman's clients included mobsters Meyer Lansky and Frank "Lefty" Rosenthal.

Oscar Goodman

Goodman's denial occurred in 1999 during his first mayoral run. He issued this denial in a statement in the midst of the colorful Las Vegas trial.

That trial involved two reputed Mafiosi charged in connection with the execution-style hit of Blitzstein, who ran rackets in Las Vegas. Goodman wasn't the only one denying the mob's Vegas existence.

Fat Herbie Blitzstein, second from left.

The first denial of the mob began in the early 1990s as part of a public relations move touting Vegas as a family friendly destination when the Nevada Gaming Commission released the first of several statements assuring the public that the FBI had forced the last of the mob out of Vegas in the 1980s.

Oscar Goodman

But that was belied by the fact that Goodman himself had represented Anthony Spilotro in a mob trial in the mid-1980's, shortly before Spilotro was killed.

What Las Vegas really needed was a white knight, and they got one in the form of Golden Nugget owner

Steve Wynn

Steve Wynn and his $630-million gamble on the Mirage. Financed mostly through the sale of junk bonds, the hotel's construction would eventually change the course of Las Vegas history.

The 1990s began with a blare of trumpets heralding the rise of a turreted medieval castle fronted by a moated drawbridge and staffed by jousting knights and fair damsels.

Excalibur reflected the 90s marketing trend to promote Las Vegas as a family-vacation destination.

Canadian circus/theater group Cirque du Soleil transformed the entertainment scene in Las Vegas with the 1993 debut of Mystere at the newly opened Treasure Island.

It would be the first of no fewer than eight Cirque shows that would launch over the next 2 decades. The era of mega hotels continued on the Strip, including the new MGM Grand hotel, backed by a full theme park, Luxor Las Vegas, and Steve Wynn's Treasure Island.

In 1993, a unique pink-domed 5-acre indoor amusement park, Grand Slam Canyon (later known as Adventuredome), became part of the Circus Circus hotel.

Fremont Street Experience

In 1995, the Fremont Street Experience was completed, revitalizing Downtown Las Vegas.

Closer to the Strip, rock restaurant magnate Peter Morton opened the Hard Rock Hotel, billed as the world's first rock and roll hotel and casino.

The year 1996 saw the advent of the French Riviera's themed Monte Carlo and the Stratosphere Las Vegas Hotel & Casino. It 1,149-foot tower makes it the highest building west of the Mississippi.

The impressive New York New York arrived in 1997.

But the surprise came in the early 2000's as Las Vegas decided to re-invent itself from a family destination to a luxury resort. Several new hotels opened, once again eclipsing anything that had come before.

Bellagio was the latest from Vegas visionary Steve Wynn, an attempt to bring grand European-style to the desert, while at the far southern end of the Strip,

Mandalay Bay Hotel Las Vegas

As if this weren't enough, the Venetian's ambitiously detailed re-creation of Venice, came along in May 1999 and was followed in short order by the opening of Paris Las Vegas in the fall of 1999.

Aladdin in Las Vegas

The 21st century opened with a bang as the Aladdin was imploded and was again transformed (which in turn only lasted for a handful of years before Planet Hollywood took it over and changed it entirely) while Steve Wynn blew up the Desert Inn and built a new showstopper named for himself.

Along the way, everyone expanded, and then expanded some more, ultimately adding thousands of new rooms. The goal became luxury with a secondary emphasis on adult fun. Little by little, wacky, eye-catching themes were phased out (as much as one can when one hotel looks like a castle), and generic sophistication took its place.

Gaming was still number one, but the newer hotels were trying to top each other in terms of other recreations: decadent nightclubs, celebrity chef backed restaurants, fancy spas, and superstar shows.

GARY JENKINS
Former Organized Crime Investigator and Mob Expert

American Mafia: *You've got one of the most popular podcasts about the mafia on the internet, The Gangland Wire. Can you tell us how it got started?*

Gary Jenkins: *In 2013 I produced a documentary and I titled it Gangland Wire. It was about this whole skimming case that started in Kansas City. I was on the task force at that time and we planted a small, hidden microphone and captured a couple of mobsters talking about Las Vegas. And we were actually trying to learn about murder plots that were being planned in a local mob war.*

Later after I'd left the investigative side of things I made a documentary about the Las Vegas Mafia because I had access to a lot of the people that worked the case I was involved with and I flew out to Las Vegas and had access to some of those other people that worked on it out there. And I really told it from a law enforcement standpoint. And after I got done with that, I was giving talks and I noticed that that people kind of like to hear me tell stories. I listened to some other podcasts and I thought, Oh, that's cool, that's fun, let me try one of those. So I figured it out and I tried a podcast, and I started out telling about the whole story behind the skim and how we got involved with investigating organized crime in Kansas City. I told stories about the mob war that we had going on at the time, and that took about four or five episodes. And then I spun off into just finding other stories about mobsters. And then I started finding former mobsters that were trying to sell books. Now they wanted to get the word out that they had a book out there and they would come on and tell their stories. And I'd find other authors that had stories, other retired FBI agents and police officers that had stories or had written books and other authors that had books.

Or just go research stories myself and tell them kind of for my own entertainment in a way because I find it fascinating. I like telling stories about big capers like the Purolater heist. That was a seven million dollar robbery in

Chicago. Or the story about the Las Vegas Hole In the Wall Gang. The night they got caught on the inside. And I just continued on with it. Gangland Wire has been going for five years now.

American Mafia: *What are some of the stories you've covered on Gangland Wire?*

Gary Jenkins: *One of the one of the more popular stories that I've covered, I made contact with a former Gambino mobster named Michael D. Leonardo, also known as Mikey Scars. He'd really only been interviewed one other time and I got a connection to him and he said, Yeah, he'd give me an interview and you know, that guy he gave me a blow by blow description of the night that he was made, and he was even better than that.*

He was made by in the Gambino family, by Sammy the Bull Gravano. And he said the reason that John Gotti, who was the boss by then, the reason John Gotti didn't conduct the ceremonies because John Gotti Jr. was going to be made that same night and he didn't feel like I feel like it was proper for John Gotti senior to be the presiding officer over the making ceremony of John Gotti Jr.

So he was made by Sammy the Bull Gravano, and he told a ton of really good mob stories, talked about Sammy the Bull, how he still talks to him all the time. And here this guy is in witness protection like he didn't want me to show his face or anything, and I kind of tried to get him back on again, but he hadn't wanted to for a while. I might have to try one more time.

Some of the other speakers and guests were retired, getting older. I had an FBI agent named Ray Morrow that worked an undercover case and on some policemen, corrupt policemen in Cleveland. That was a really two or three year-long case. That was really fascinating.

I was able to get Joe Pistone on there, the original Donnie Brasco character, one of the more fun stories I did. I have another guy, a local guy in Kansas City that served about 12 years in the Federal system and we got to know each other and we're still friends today.

He got hold of me and he knows about the podcast. He likes to listen to it and he knows a lot of mob guys himself. And he said, he'd heard Joe Pistone talking about how he would hate to be the cellmate of Lefty Rogerio and Lefty Rogerio was kind of his rabbi, his stick... his pal that introduced him into the Sonny Black Napolitano crew which was a Bonanno family-affiliated crew in New York City.

I have another retired FBI agent named Doug Penso, who was a friend of mine, worked in Kansas City for a while. And Doug was the guy that went to Lefty Rogerio and Sonny Black Napolitano and told them that Joe Pistone - Donnie Brasco - was not really a thief. He was not really a criminal. He was an FBI agent named Joe Pistone and showed a picture of Joe Pistone with a bunch of FBI agents that they knew to prove that he was really an FBI agent because they were afraid they were going to put a hit out on him.

Through booms and busts, recessions and pandemics, Las Vegas has always sprung back. With legitimate corporations running the hotels and government regulators policing the gaming licensing process Las Vegas has regained an air of sophistication and respectability that is a far cry from its early days as a mob run town. But some speculate the future of Las Vegas is very much in question.

As the COVID-19 pandemic crippled Las Vegas and the world economy, what is the future of Las Vegas? Financial analysts say the city is poised for a spectacular resurgence, while naysayers say it is the beginning of the end for this glittering jewel box in the desert.

But just as we may have thought organized crime was over in Las Vegas, a new and more sinister element has taken its place. Gone are the Dons and Lieutenants of old, only to be replaced by organized crime elements transnational in their origin and reach.

According to the FBI, Drug cartels have changed the landscape and altered the way Mafia groups operate.

The days of scheming with labor unions to skim money from contracts are all but gone, but a new breed of criminal in Las Vegas and other major American cities still rely on some of the same racketeering scams they always have: selling drugs, and trafficking firearms, humans and counterfeit goods. Add to these...credit card scams, money laundering, internet fraud and other racketeering scams made easier in the digital age.

How these new groups are altering the ever-changing landscape of law and order in Las Vegas is a Chapter yet to be written.

Chapter 10:

THE LAST RESORT - THE FINAL CHAPTER?
♠

The story of Las Vegas is a fairy tale of immense improbability, one that belies even the strangest of fictions. But as truth is often stranger than fiction, Las Vegas is the unbelievable story of how one small speck in the desert became a glittering metropolis of hedonism. But it's also one more story in the chapter that organized crime played in the building and bilking of the American Dream.

Public interest in the subject of the mafia's control over Las Vegas has never waned. Many books have been written about those years by both associates of the mob and the members of the law enforcement agencies involved in apprehending them.

Before his death from COVID-19 at the age of 81, former gangster-turned informant Frank Cullotta wrote his book titled: "Cullotta: The Life of a Chicago Criminal, Las Vegas Mobster and Government Witness."

Frank Cullotta's book is just one of hundreds which continue to be published, proving the public's insatiable hunger for hearing the story of organized crime.

The public interest has never waned since the early years when city newspapers shouted headlines about the latest mob hits while outlining in lurid detail law enforcement's relentless pursuit of justice.

ERIC DEZENBALL

American Mafia: *You've written a semi-fictional book with some Las Vegas mob characters in it. Can you tell us a little bit more about it?*

Eric Dezenhall: *My book is called The Devil Himself. It is historical fiction. It is based on the true story of Meyer Lansky, whose involvement in World War Two, his partnership with the U.S. Navy to help guard the ports of New York to prevent Nazi sabotage. And there had been sabotage, both Nazi and other types of sabotage in and around New York. U-boats were spotted in the Hudson River and as part of what was called Operation Underworld, Luciano Lucky Luciano and Meyer Lansky helped the Navy find contacts in Sicily to help plan for the allied invasion.*

There's a lot of mythology around Operation Underworld. On one hand, you will have people tell you that it was a swindle nothing ever happened. That's not true, nor is it true with the opposite end that Lucky Luciano Lucky Luciano came storming ashore with General Patton's army, but the mob did play to play a significant role in helping guard the ports and helping to make it inhospitable for Nazi sympathizers. And as a result, Lucky Luciano was 30 to 50 year sentence for pandering was commuted and he was deported to Italy not long after World War Two ended.

American Mafia: *Where can our readers find the book?*

Eric Dezenhall: *My book is available at Amazon and also Barnes and Noble.*

THE MOB MUSEUM

On February 14, 2012 the National Museum of Organized Crime and Law Enforcement opened in Downtown Las Vegas. The Mob Museum is dedicated to featuring the artifacts, stories, and history of organized crime in the United States, as well as the actions and initiatives by law enforcement to prevent such crimes. The museum is housed in the former Las Vegas Post Office and Courthouse, which was built in 1933 and is listed on the National Register of Historic Places. The museum is located on Stewart Avenue, two blocks north of Fremont Street, the main artery of the downtown casino district.

Developed under the creative direction of Dennis Barrie, co-creator of the International Spy Museum and the Rock and Roll Hall of Fame, the museum is governed by a non-profit board, the "300 Stewart Avenue Corporation," in partnership with the City of Las Vegas. The museum is dedicated to the contentious relationship between organized crime and law enforcement within the historical context of Las Vegas and the entire United States.

MICHAEAL GREEN ON THE MOB MUSEUM

American Mafia: *What is the Mob Museum and how did it get its start?*

Michael Green: *The Mob Museum is one of the more popular and respected museums now in the U.S., and I take a little pride in that. I worked on it, though I'm not going to claim ownership.*

The building was the Federal courthouse, which included every kind of Federal operation when it opened in nineteen thirty three. And as time went on, they moved everything out until there was very little left. And the Federal government was going to close it and knock it down.

Oscar Goodman had become mayor, and he said, "Wait a minute. I tried my first case there. I threw up on the courthouse steps. We can't lose this old building."

Now, if you think about it, Las Vegas has the reputation for imploding buildings. Actually, the buildings that are imploded are older strip hotels that unfortunately, you know, I hate to see the buildings go. They can't compete with the modern hotels.

A Federal building is a different thing. Well, the Federal government said, OK, you want the building, we'll give it to you pretty much. But it has to be cultural. And Goodman really supported the idea of a museum about organized crime, and they did studies. What should we do?

They interviewed people, and eventually it did come around to a museum of organized crime and law enforcement. Now the curators who did it originally, Dennis and Kathy Barrie, also had done the Rock and Roll Hall of Fame in the International Spy Museum, which because of the subject matter.

Their museums, but their attraction. And that's what the Mob Museum would be, too. Now I say we because I'm involved with the content, we have had to redo a lot of things, whether material no longer was available to us or new things came out or simply having to change with the times.

But the museum opened on Valentine's Day 2012, and the day mattered because one of the key attractions is the wall from the St. Valentine's Day massacre. And the museum has gone on over the next decade to be very popular, to be involved in the community, presenting programs on law enforcement, but also trying to give you both sides. It does not glorify organized crime in the least.

At the same time, when we were working on it, we had law enforcement officials have said, you know, you also have to make sure you don't make us out to be perfect, which they weren't. And the museum conveys that.

So the goal of the museum is to educate you and entertain you and inform you. And as any museum or documentary ought to do, teach you something. Have you walk away from it after visiting and have you say "Where can I find out more?"

American Mafia: *What can visitors expect to learn and experience when they attend the Mob Museum and see its exhibits?*

Michael Green: *I think if you go to the museum and you go from top to bottom because you start on the third floor and then go down, you should learn how organized crime evolved or devolved as the case may be, how law* enforcement had to adapt and change, but also how Las Vegas evolved through time from this sleepy little town that depended mainly on the railroad to becoming an international tourist capital.

Each floor kind of deals with a period not so much a theme. There are several themes on each one, but I think that when you're done, you have found out a good deal about how organized crime rose and fell in terms of its power.

How Las Vegas rose to the heights. And some would say the issues that it has today, but also the history of American law enforcement, local and national, because everything from the FBI to local law enforcement appears in it.

Then you could go to the basement and go to the speakeasy, and yes, you can get drinks and all that. And the museum has its own distillery and as an example of how things happened with the museum.

There's a flask in the distillery that I found at the Pasadena flea market, and I took photos of it and texted it to our curators and said, Does this look like it's a 20th flask? And we agreed it did OK. I bought it. We took a flyer. They researched it. Yeah, it's from the prohibition era. So we bought it and included that.

What you also have in there are some dresses. The students at UNLV who study history and public history, museums and the like did an exhibit on prohibition era fashion, and the museum includes some of the material they found, including what my wife found at an estate sale.

And this is what happens with museums. People come in with material, say, "Is this something?" And sometimes it is, and sometimes it isn't. And when it is, it's a great feeling.

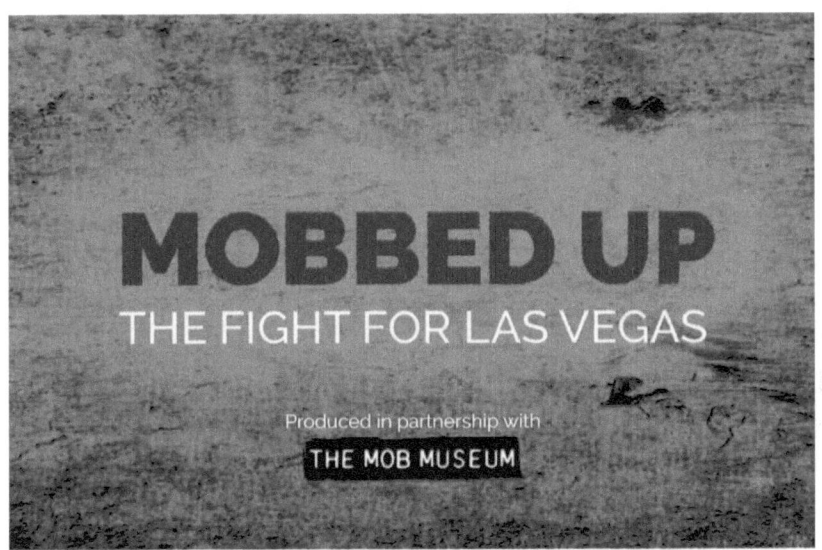

The Mob Museum also produced the program 'Mobbed Up: The Fight for Las Vegas,' an 11-part true-crime podcast series produced by the Las Vegas Review-Journal in partnership with The Mob Museum, chronicles the mob's rise and fall in Las Vegas through the eyes of those who lived it: ex-mobsters, law enforcement officials, politicians and journalists.

In telling both sides of the story, history cannot forget the brave men and women of law enforcement who worked tirelessly to bring justice to the streets of Las Vegas.

The FBI, in conjunction with the Las Vegas Metro Task force, were instrumental in bringing ruthless criminals to trial and getting convictions to stand.

But the story could not be complete without praise for the broadcast journalists and crime reporters in the media that were willing to risk their lives to bring the truth to the people.

Though mob influence and control has left Las Vegas, what will happen to this city of Sin? Las Vegas has a history of survival and resilience, and it's likely it will re-emerge as one of the greatest success stories in history. But never forget its humble beginnings, a place that may never have come into existence without The American Mafia.

APPENDIX I
♠

Members of the U.S. Senate Special Committee to Investigate Organized Crime in Interstate Commerce (Kefauver Committee) are shown left to right: Charles W. Tobey (NH), Lester C. Hunt (WY), Estes Kefauver (TN), Alexander Wiley (WI), Herbert R. O'Conor (MD) - *Photo from U.S. Senate archives.*

THE KEFAUVER COMMITTEE

In the aftermath of World War II, the public started hearing more about organized crime and its corrosive influence in communities across America. Business and political leaders demanded action. A freshman U.S. senator from Tennessee, Estes

Kefauver, seized the opportunity. In 1950 and 1951, he chaired a Senate committee charged with investigating organized crime and exposing its corruption of public institutions. The Kefauver Committee held hearings in 14 cities across the country, including one in the courtroom of this building. The Kefauver hearings confirmed the existence of a national crime syndicate and revealed lax enforcement.

Special Committee on Organized Crime in Interstate Commerce

Senator Estes Kefauver of Tennessee

(The Kefauver Committee)

Resolution passed: May 2, 1950.

Chairman:

C. Estes Kefauver 1950-1951; Herbert O'Conor 1951

Committee members:

Lester Hunt (D-WY)

Herbert O'Conor (D-MD)

Charles Tobey (R-NH)

Alexander Wiley (R-WI)

Origins

In 1949 the American Municipal Association, representing more than 10,000 cities nationwide, petitioned the Federal government to combat the growing influence of organized crime. First-term senator Estes Kefauver of Tennessee drafted a resolution to create a special committee to investigate the issue. The Commerce and Judiciary Committees battled to control the investigation, and following a protracted debate, Vice President Alben Barkley cast the tie-breaking vote to establish a special committee.

Process

Senate Resolution 202 provided the Special Committee on Organized Crime in Interstate Commerce, commonly known as the Kefauver Committee, with $150,000 to study interstate crime. When the five-member committee was set to expire at the end of February 1951, the public inundated Congress with letters demanding that the inquiry continue. The Senate responded, extending support for the investigation to September 1, 1951. During the course of the 15-month investigation, the committee met in 14 major U.S. cities and interviewed hundreds of witnesses in open and executive session.

Public Relations

Though not the first congressional committee to televise its proceedings, the Kefauver Committee hearings became the most widely viewed congressional investigation to date. An estimated 30 million Americans tuned in to watch the live proceedings in March 1951. The television broadcasts educated a broad audience about the complicated issues of interstate crime. "Television and radio make these events more vivid and alive to the general public than newspapers," explained one New York teacher. "I do not think any of you can possibly realize how much good it has done to have these hearings televised," wrote Mrs. Carl Johnson. "It has made millions of us aware of conditions that we would never have fully realized even if we had read the newspaper accounts."

The broadcasts made the Kefauver Committee a household name; in March 1951, 72 percent of Americans were familiar with the Kefauver Committee's work. Schools dismissed students to watch the hearings. Blood banks ran low on donations, prompting one Brooklyn Center to install a television and tune in to the hearings, and donations shot up 100 percent. "Never before had the attention of the nation been riveted so completely on a single matter," explained Life magazine. "The Senate investigation into interstate crime," it concluded, "was almost the sole subject of national conversation."

In December 1951 Americans selected Chairman Kefauver as one of 10 most admired men, joining a list of notables including Pope Pius XII, Albert Einstein, and Douglas MacArthur. Kefauver sought the Democratic Party presidential nomination in 1952 and 1956. Though he was unsuccessful in his bid for the presidency, in 1956 Democrats selected Kefauver as their vice presidential candidate. The Adlai Stevenson-Kefauver ticket lost the election to incumbents Dwight Eisenhower and Richard Nixon.

Investigation

Building upon the earlier work of state crime commissions, Kefauver directed committee staff to examine what he called "the life blood of organized crime": interstate gambling. Investigating gambling, according to one scholar, "meant that Kefauver and his colleagues first focused on urban areas, the strongholds of both gangsters and Democrats." Despite the potential political cost to his party, Kefauver pledged to lead a "no stones unturned, no holds barred, right down the middle of the road, let the chips fall where they may" inquiry.

The committee launched its investigation in Miami on May 28, 1950, and found evidence of gambling everywhere, from restaurants to cigar stands. The committee traced one bookmaking syndicate's political connections all the way to Florida governor Fuller Warren, a Democrat. Warren accused

Kefauver of being an "ambition-crazed Caesar who is trying desperately and futilely" to be a presidential candidate. The committee's summary, which implicated the governor in illicit gambling activities, proved to be Warren's political downfall.

In Kansas City, the committee confronted, in Kefauver's words, a "place that was struggling out from under the rule of the law of the jungle." In Chicago, the committee heard testimony from gangsters who confessed to using legitimate business interests to curry favor with local law enforcement. Revelations of bribery and illegal gambling among the city's police force drew intense scrutiny from the mayor, leading one journalist to report that "one-fifth of the city's police captains were said to be slated for the skids." The Chicago investigation connected top officials—most of whom were members of the Democratic Party—with corrupt practices. Many Illinois Democrats lost their reelection bids in that year's midterm election, including Senate Majority Leader Scott Lucas. During his final months in office, a bitter Lucas tried unsuccessfully to prematurely end the committee's investigation.

Public interest in the Kefauver inquiry peaked in March 1951 when the committee convened hearings in New York City and millions of Americans watched the live broadcast. The televised hearings became, in the words of Senator Kefauver, "a national crusade, a great debating forum, an arouser of public opinion on the state of the nation's morals." Viewers watched incredulously as a cadre of individuals representing the underworld of interstate bookmaking and gambling interests offered details of their sordid business arrangements. Criminals "as suave and well-mannered as their investigators," observed one journalist, "were treated with the courtesy customarily reserved for law-abiding citizens." Kefauver's studied and balanced approach to his witnesses earned him the respect of many Americans.

Television viewers were riveted, in part, by the cast of characters called to testify before the committee. Particularly dramatic was testimony by Frank Costello. Crime commissions across the nation had identified Costello as a key figure in the nation's largest gambling syndicates. Testifying before the committee in New York, Costello, with his well-coiffed hair and tailored suits, came to personify the American gangster in public imagination. When his legal counsel objected to the television cameras, cameramen instead directed their devices at Costello's hands. During an intense period of questioning by Rudolph Halley, Costello's hands "twisted and clenched," according to one account, "revealing [his] inner fears and confusion." Costello mumbled incoherent answers, became belligerent, refused to answer questions, and twice left the witness table without being dismissed. Americans were fascinated by the spectacle of a mob boss under duress. The committee later cited him for contempt and he served jail time.

In addition to Costello, the committee interrogated a veritable who's who of the criminal underworld. Virginia Hill Hauser, former girlfriend of criminal mastermind Bugsy Siegel, testified to having had no knowledge of criminal activities while in the company of notorious mobsters. Antagonized by the press, Hill kicked and slapped aggressive journalists on her way out of the hearing room, actions caught on live television. Former New York City mayor William O'Dwyer testified to allegations of corruption during his tenure. Then serving as ambassador to Mexico, O'Dwyer's answers lacked specificity, leading the public to conclude that he was being intentionally evasive. The committee initiated perjury action against him. His reputation shattered, O'Dwyer resigned his diplomatic post.

Outcome

The committee's legislative achievements were modest, at best. Kefauver favored the creation of a Federal Crime Commission, which the FBI and Department of Justice ardently opposed. The committee's second chairman, Herbert O'Conor (who took over after an exhausted Kefauver stepped down as chairman), sponsored legislation aimed at controlling illegal drugs by expanding appropriations for the Narcotics Bureau, the committee's sole legislative accomplishment.

More important were the non-legislative results of the investigation. By bringing public opinion to bear on the problems of interstate crime, the investigation helped local and state law enforcement and elected officials to aggressively pursue criminal syndicates. The hearings clearly demonstrated that some elected officials had facilitated and profited from criminal activities. These dramatic hearings also made certain that television would play a large role in future Senate investigations.

APPENDIX II
♠

VIRGINIA HILL

Virginia Hill's relationship with Bugsy Siegel has long been debated. It was in her Beverly Hills home where Bugsy was murdered, though she was reportedly out of the country at the time of the killing. In 1951, she was subpoenaed to testify before the Kefauver hearings, where she denied having any knowledge of organized crime despite being described by Time magazine in March of that year as the "queen of the gangsters' molls."

Virginia Hill
Virginia Hill Hauser Testimony Transcript -
SELECTED EXCERPTS
From: Hearings Part 7: New York-New Jersey

The Chairman: Regarding the Flamingo Hotel. Did you spend a good deal of time there with Ben Siegel?

Mrs. Hauser: Yes.

The Chairman: Do you recall the instance where he had trouble with some other people about spending too much money, of the Flamingos?

Mrs. Hauser: No. The only time I ever saw him, he was pacing the floor up and down, was because the way, I don't know, sometimes at night, he said that lie had lost, or I don't know what was the matter. But I told him, why did he want to stay in that thing like that if it was worrying him so, because he seemed to be awful worried about the business. And he couldn't get the kitchen running right, and all that stuff. He said everything was upside down.

The Chairman: Did he have Moe Sedway as manager, or something like that?

Mrs. Hauser: Moe Sedway wasn't around there.

The Chairman: Moe Sedway came from Rosen, didn't he?

Mrs. Hauser: I don't know about that. I don't think Moe Sedway had anything to do with the Flamingo when I was there.

The Chairman: You knew Moe Sedway, didn't you?

Mrs. Hauser: I knew Moe Sedway, yes.

The Chairman: Then this chap that came out from New York to take over the Flamingo after Ben Siegel was killed, do you know him?

Mrs. Hauser: Well, you see, I know nothing about it. I haven't been around, I haven't got in touch with those people, I know nothing about it.

The Chairman: Did you go back to California when you came back from Reno?

Mrs. Hauser: From Reno, when I was looking for a ranch, I went to San Francisco. Then I caught a plane. 1 wanted to do some shopping for my baby, and then I went back to Spokane, and I was never around any of those people any more.

The Chairman: So you haven't been back to Los Angeles since then?

Mrs. Hauser: No.

The Chairman: Did you have a home in Los Angeles or Beverly Hills?

Mrs. Hauser: No; I never had a home there. You mean owned it? No.

The Chairman: Where did you live in Los Angeles?

Mrs. Hauser: I lived? At the time I lived on Linden Drive — I don't remember the number — where Ben was killed.

The Chairman: That was your home, where he was killed?

Mrs. Hauser: It wasn't my home. It was Mr. Romero's home.

The Chairman: I know, but you had it rented, didn't you?

Mrs. Hauser: Ben rented it, I don't know, or my brother — I don't know who used to pay. I think they paid him $500 a month, but Ben gave the money to pay him.

The Chairman: That was Mr. Romero?

Mrs. Hauser: Yes.

The Chairman: What was his first name?

Mrs. Hauser: Juan.

The Chairman: How long did you have that house?

Mrs. Hauser: Well, it wasn't so long.

The Chairman: But Ben rented the house from him and then you and your brother lived there; is that the situation?

Mrs. Hauser: Yes.

The Chairman: And your brother and Allen Smiley were there when he was killed?

Mrs. Hauser: Yes, and this other girl that worked for me.

The Chairman: And a girl who worked for you?

Mrs. Hauser: Yes.

The Chairman: You mean a servant in the house?

Mrs. Hauser: Well, she used to run errands, you know, buy my things and fix my hair and everything.

The Chairman: Sort of a secretary and what not?

Mrs. Hauser: Yes.

The Chairman: What was her name?

Mrs. Hauser: Jerrie.

The Chairman: How well did you know Allen Smiley?

Mrs. Hauser: Well, he was around all the time With Ben.

The Chairman: Was he a good friend?

Mrs. Hauser: Yes.

The Chairman: Did Ben have much to say about his wire-service difficulties he was having at that time?

Mrs. Hauser: I never heard anything about the wire service. One time I was going to read something in the Time magazine, I saw his picture, and he took it away from me.

The Chairman: He wouldn't let you know about it?

Mrs. Hauser: No.

The Chairman: Didn't that arouse your suspicion that he wanted to keep that a secret from you?

Mrs. Hauser: Well, he told me I had no business knowing that, don't read that, and everything, so-

The Chairman: He didn't usually just jerk things away from you; did he?

Mrs. Hauser: He did. I was in an airport with him in Las Vegas, and I saw it, but he wouldn't let me read it.

The Chairman: But when you were just reading a newspaper, he wouldn't do that to you, would he?

Mrs. Hauser: Well, there was never much about him in the newspaper.

The Chairman: Anyway, he didn't want you to know about his wire-service difficulties?

Mrs. Hauser: He didn't want me evidently to know about anything.

The Chairman: Why did you think that was so?

Mrs. Hauser: I don't know.

The Chairman: Well, particularly when he saw that you were reading in a magazine about his difficulty with the wire service, he jerked Time magazine out of your hand; is that true?

Mrs. Hauser: Yes.

The Chairman: What did he say about it then?

Mrs. Hauser: He said, "Don't read that baloney."

The Chairman: He just didn't want you to believe that he had had any difficulty about the wire service isn't that it?

Mrs. Hauser: Well, I don't know anything about a wire service myself.

The Chairman: Do you feel like talking about it? Do you have any theory about what happened, who it was had it in for him? I don't want you to mention any name.

Mrs. Hauser: Mr. Kefauver, if I knew anything about it, believe me, I would be the first one to talk. I don't know anything, and I have asked people and they say they don't know anything. Nobody seems to know anything.

The Chairman: Did he and Allen Smiley seem to be very good friends?

Mrs. Hauser: He was very good to Smiley and he was always — they were always together, and Smiley was always around.

Mr. Halley: Just one thing. Mrs. Houser, you have testified now about a lot of details of your own finances and your own business.

The Chairman: Mrs. Hauser you must have heard about the business of Siegel, or Adonis?

Mrs. Hauser: I never knew anything about their business. They didn't tell me about their business. Why would they tell me? I don't care anything about business in the first place. I don't even understand it.

RECOMMENDED READING
♠

Las Vegas Babylon: True Tales of Glitter, Glamour, and Greed
by Jeff Burbank

Lost Las Vegas
by Jeff Burbank

Las Vegas: A Centennial History
by Michael Green

Bringing Down Cullotta
by Dennis N. Griffin and David Bowman

Howard Hughes: Power, Paranoia, and Palace Intrigue, Revised and Expanded (Volume 1)
by Geoff Schumacher

Leaving Vegas: How FBI Wiretaps Ended Mob Domination of Las Vegas Casinos
by Gary Jenkins

Being Oscar: From Mob Lawyer to Mayor of Las Vegas
by Oscar Goodman

Of Rats and Men: Oscar Goodman's Life from Mob Mouthpiece to Mayor of Las Vegas
by John L. Smith

The Devil Himself: A Novel
by Eric Dezenhall

The Rise and Fall of a 'Casino' Mobster: The Tony Spilotro Story Through a Hitman's Eyes
by Frank Cullottta and Dennis N. Griffin

The Battle for Las Vegas: The Law vs. The Mob
By Dennis Griffin

Mob Lawyer: Including the Inside Account of Who Killed Jimmy Hoffa and JFK
by Frank Ragano (Author), Selwyn Raab (Author), Nicholas Pileggi (Foreword)

INDEX
♠

Addison, 16
Adlai Stevenson, 171
Aiuppa, 108, 109, 111
Aladdin, 54, 113, 150
Argent, 73, 87
Balistrieri, 76, 80, 82
Bank of Las Vegas, 64
Barbra Streisand, 60, 61
Barrie, 160, 162
Batista, 45
Bellagio, 139, 149
Berman, 33
Blitzstein, 90, 96, 119, 120, 145
Bobby Kennedy, 48, 105
Brancato, 40
Caesars Palace, 54, 60
Calabrese, 112
California, 11, 26, 128, 178
Carlisi, 108
Castaways, 73
Chagra, 96
Chicago, 31, 40, 46, 65, 74, 79, 81, 85, 86, 97, 104, 107, 108, 109, 111, 112, 116, 120, 153, 157, 172
Circus Circus, 85, 148
Cirque du Soleil, 119, 147
Civella, 46, 47, 104

Cleveland Mayfield Road Gang, 63
Coppola, 133
Costello, 38, 173, 174
D'Arco, 135
Dalitz, 61, 62, 63, 64, 73
David Bowman, 4, 186
Davino, 91
Dean Martin, 36, 53, 57
Democrats, 171, 172
Dennis Griffin, 5, 187
Desert Inn, 62, 63, 64, 72, 150
Detra, 12, 13, 14, 15
Dezenhall, 31, 38, 39, 63, 140, 158, 160, 187
Dinah Shore, 52
Don Rickles, 56
East Coast mob, 30
El Cortez Hotel, 26
El Rancho, 9, 15, 16, 20, 116
Elvis Presley, 36
FBI, 5, 79, 81, 83, 84, 86, 93, 111, 134, 137, 140, 146, 152, 154, 155, 156, 164, 166, 174, 186
Fidel Castro, 45
Flamingo, 10, 20, 21, 22, 23, 26, 27, 28, 29, 30, 31, 33, 40, 42, 177, 178

Frank Sinatra, 36, 52, 53, 56, 57, 125
Fremont Hotel, 73
French Riviera, 149
Frontier Hotel, 126
Gary Jenkins, 5, 151, 153, 186
Genovese, 133, 134, 135, 137, 138
George Raft, 27
George Sanders, 27
Giancana, 46, 48, 49
Gigante, 135, 137
Goffstein, 33
Golden Nugget, 11, 15, 115, 130, 132, 133, 147
Goodman, 95, 96, 97, 99, 101, 103, 144, 145, 146, 161, 162, 186, 187
Gotti, 153
Greenbaum, 31, 33, 39, 40, 41, 42, 43
Guardino, 91
Hacienda, 73, 76, 85
Highway 91, 8, 12, 13
Hole in the Wall Gang, 86, 88, 91, 111
Howard Hughes, 69, 70, 71, 128, 129, 140, 186
Jackie Sharon, 111
JEFF BURBANK, 67, 81, 120
JENKINS, 111, 151
Jessel, 27
Jimmy Durante, 27, 51, 52
Jimmy Hoffa, 65, 66, 67, 187

Joe Blasko, 91
Joe E. Lewis, 51
Joe Pesci, 89, 98
John Kennedy, 57
Kefauver, 44, 167, 168, 169, 170, 171, 172, 174, 176, 184
Klawitter, 13
Korsak, 31, 32
Kurland, 16
Landmark Hotel, 73
Lanksy, 19, 35
Larry Henry, 5, 87, 103, 104, 115
LARRY HENRY, 86, 103, 114
Las Vegas Boulevard, 16
Las Vegas Club, 16
Last Frontier, 9, 11
Leonetti, 96
Liberace, 59
Lisner, 94
Lombardozzi, 138
Louis Prima, 56
Luciano, 36, 38, 45, 64, 133, 158
Mafia, 1, 2, 1, 4, 9, 10, 11, 15, 18, 20, 21, 22, 33, 37, 42, 43, 46, 54, 57, 67, 73, 84, 86, 87, 103, 104, 109, 110, 113, 114, 115, 118, 122, 125, 128, 135, 136, 151, 153, 156, 158, 160, 161, 163, 166
Mandalay Bay, 139, 149
Marlene Dietrich, 59
Matecki, 91
Maurice Friedman, 125
McAfee, 11, 14, 15, 16

McCarthy, 94, 95
McGee, 81, 92
MICHAEL GREEN, 9, 20, 37, 42, 54, 76, 99, 109, 130
Milton Berle, 51
Milton Farmer Page, 16
Mirage, 113, 114, 115, 119, 123, 124, 130, 147
Miraglia, 94, 95
Mob Museum, 5, 117, 160, 161, 162, 163, 166
Mobbed Up, 166
Moelis, 16
Moldea, 69, 89
Monte Carlo, 149
Mormon Church, 36
Napolitano, 155
Narcotics Bureau, 174
Neumann, 91
Nevada Gaming, 79, 145
New Frontier, 35, 73, 126
Ocean's Eleven, 53, 57
Operation Family Secrets, 112
Operation Underworld, 158
Pair-O-Dice Club, 12
Peter Lawford, 53, 57
Pietra, 111
Pileggi, 89, 187
Pioneer Club, 16
Pistone, 154, 155
Princeton University, 36
prohibition, 9, 10, 16, 17, 42, 165

Provenzano, 68, 69
race wire, 20, 26
Rat Pack, 52, 53, 57, 139
Red Rooster, 13, 14
Richard Nixon, 67, 171
RICO, 105, 136, 141
Riviera, 35, 42, 59
Robert Kennedy, 48
Rogerio, 154, 155
Romero, 179, 180
Rosenthal, 75, 76, 77, 78, 79, 80, 81, 82, 85, 87, 88, 89, 92, 96, 99, 100, 104, 111, 116, 118, 144
Sahara, 9, 16, 35, 56, 59, 88, 91
Salerno, 133, 134, 135, 136, 137, 138
Sammy Davis Jr, 57
Sands, 35, 53, 57, 73, 131
Scarfo, 96
Scherer, 16
Sedway, 26, 31, 33, 42, 44, 177, 178
Selwynn Raab, 5
Sharon Stone, 89, 92
Siegel, 18, 19, 20, 21, 22, 23, 24, 25, 26, 27, 28, 29, 30, 31, 32, 33, 38, 42, 43, 174, 176, 177, 178, 184
Siegfried and Roy, 55, 77, 118
Silver Slipper, 73
Sophie Tucker, 51
Sorvino, 138

Spilotro, 79, 81, 83, 84, 85, 86, 87, 88, 89, 92, 93, 94, 95, 96, 97, 98, 104, 106, 107, 108, 109, 110, 111, 112, 113, 116, 118, 120, 144, 146, 187

Stardust, 52, 55, 64, 73, 74, 76, 81, 85, 87, 96, 113, 116

Stardust Hotel, 52

Steve Wynn, 113, 115, 124, 125, 126, 129, 130, 132, 133, 144, 147, 148, 149, 150

Stratosphere, 149

Summit Meeting, 53

Sunset Strip, 12, 28

Teamsters, 64, 65, 66, 74, 76, 136

the Marina, 74, 76

the Outfit, 81, 85

Thunderbird, 16, 42

Tony the Ant, 81, 85, 86, 97

Trombino, 40

Tufts, 27

Union Pacific Railroad, 9

Vegas Vic, 16

Virginia Hill, 22, 29, 32, 174, 176, 177

Wilbur Clark, 63

Wilkerson, 21, 28, 29

William O'Dwyer, 174

Xavier Cugat, 27

www.ingramcontent.com/pod-product-compliance
Lightning Source LLC
Chambersburg PA
CBHW030151100526
44592CB00009B/215